chess psychology

approaching the psychological battle both on and off the board

ANGUS DUNNINGTON

EVERYMAN CHESS

Gloucester Publishers plc   www.everymanchess.com

First published in 2003 by Gloucester Publishers plc (formerly Everyman Publishers plc), Gloucester Mansions, 140A Shaftesbury Avenue, London WC2H 8HD

British Library Cataloguing-in-Publication Data
A catalogue record for this book is available from the British Library.

ISBN 1 85744 326 8

Distributed in North America by The Globe Pequot Press, P.O Box 480, 246 Goose Lane, Guilford, CT 06437-0480.

All other sales enquiries should be directed to Everyman Chess, Gloucester Publishers plc, Gloucester Mansions, 140A Shaftesbury Avenue, London WC2H 8HD
tel: 020 7539 7600 fax: 020 7379 4060
email: info@everymanchess.com
website: www.everymanchess.com

Everyman is the registered trade mark of Random House Inc. and is used in this work under license from Random House Inc.

EVERYMAN CHESS SERIES (formerly Cadogan Chess)
Chief advisor: Garry Kasparov
Commissioning editor: Byron Jacobs

Typeset and edited by First Rank Publishing, Brighton.
Cover design by Horatio Monteverde.
Production by Navigator Guides.
Printed and bound in Great Britain by Biddles Ltd.

Everyman Chess

Popular opening books:

1 85744 218 0	Unusual QG Declined	Chris Ward
1 85744 253 9	Alekhine's Defence	Nigel Davies
1 85744 256 4	Queen's Gambit Declined	Matthew Sadler
1 85744 232 6	French Classical	Byron Jacobs
1 85744 281 4	Modern Defence	Speelman & McDonald
1 85744 292 X	Symmetrical English	David Cummings
1 85744 290 3	c3 Sicilian	Joe Gallagher
1 85744 242 3	Offbeat Spanish	Glenn Flear
1 85744 262 8	Classical Nimzo-Indian	Bogdan Lalic
1 85744 291 1	Sicilian Grand Prix Attack	James Plaskett
1 85744 252 0	Dutch Stonewall	Jacob Aagaard
1 85744 257 1	Sicilian Kalashnikov	Pinski & Aagaard
1 85744 276 8	French Winawer	Neil McDonald

Books for players serious about improving their game:

1 85744 226 1	Starting Out in Chess	Byron Jacobs
1 85744 231 8	Tips for Young Players	Matthew Sadler
1 85744 236 9	Improve Your Opening Play	Chris Ward
1 85744 241 5	Improve Your Middlegame Play	Andrew Kinsman
1 85744 246 6	Improve Your Endgame Play	Glenn Flear
1 85744 223 7	Mastering the Opening	Byron Jacobs
1 85744 228 8	Mastering the Middlegame	Angus Dunnington
1 85744 233 4	Mastering the Endgame	Glenn Flear
1 85744 238 5	Simple Chess	John Emms

Books for the more advanced player:

1 85744 233 4	Attacking with 1 e4	John Emms
1 85744 233 4	Attacking with 1 d4	Angus Dunnington
1 85744 219 9	Meeting 1 e4	Alexander Raetsky
1 85744 224 5	Meeting 1 d4	Aagaard and Lund
1 85744 273 3	Excelling at Chess	Jacob Aagaard

chess psychology

approaching the psychological battle both on and off the board

ANGUS DUNNINGTON

EVERYMAN CHESS

Gloucester Publishers plc www.everymanchess.com

CONTENTS

Bibliography and Acknowledgements

Books (chess)
Chess Brilliancy, Iakov Damsky (Everyman 2002)
Chess: The search for the Mona Lisa, Eduard Gufeld (Batsford 2001)
I Play Against Pieces, Svetozar Gligoric (Batsford 2002)
Khalifman: Life & Games, Gennedy Nesis (Everyman 2002)
Shall We Play Fischerandom Chess?, Svetozar Gligoric (Batsford 2002)
The Art of Chess Analysis, Jan Timman (Cadogan 1997)
The Life and Games of Mikhail Tal, Mikhail Tal (Cadogan 1997)

Books (psychology)
Cognitive Psychology, Michael W. Eysenck & Mark T. Keane (Psychology Press 2000)
Great Sporting Quotations, David Pickering (Past Times 2002)
Principles of Cognitive Psychology, Michael W. Eysenck (Psychology Press 1999)
Principles of Social Psychology, Nicky Hayes (Psychology Press 2000)
Problem Solving, Hank Kahney (Open University Press 1999)
The Making of Intelligence, Ken Richardson (Phoenix 2000)
Understanding Psychology, Robert S. Feldman (McGraw-Hill 1993)

Periodicals
Informator
Chessbase Magazine

Acknowledgements
As usual I would like to thank Byron Jacobs for his patience, and an extra special acknowledgement should go to my wife, Mioto who, apart from being a computer engineer, linguist and mother of our 16-month old daughter, Mia, is also a paid up, qualified member of The British Psychological Society. Her help with some of the finer aspects of psychology made a difference.

INTRODUCTION

'Chess is a sad waste of brains.'
Sir Walter Scott

Psychology is the scientific study of behaviour and mental processes. Of course the subject of psychology is vast, featuring thoughts, feelings, perceptions, reasoning processes, memories and so on, these being major factors in determining how we play chess and with what degree of success.

There's a tournament coming up later in the month and you want to do well. You buy a few chess books, perhaps even a shiny new chess set to mark a new beginning. You learn some theory, browse through a few dozen games on a computer database, solve a handful of puzzles to sharpen up your tactical awareness, perform as many as three full physical training sessions – each consisting of no less than five press-ups – and *hey presto* – let the games begin! You're ready to go into battle with the energy of Kasparov, the youth and ambition of Radjabov, the confidence and composure of Kramnik, the wizard-like magic of Tal, the speed of Anand...

In the first round everything goes according to plan and you're playing the part well, impressing yourself, your opponent and any passing spectators. Right up to the fourth move, in fact. At that point your opponent chooses an offbeat path that you hardly bothered looking at when learning the theory in view of its dubious reputation and, after your initial ambitious expectations subside, you simply lose direction, unable to get to grips with the situation. And it's all downhill from there. The rest of the tournament is a catalogue of hard luck stories, ranging from blundering away a full point when your opponent – also yet to score – was really insulting your intelligence playing on, to walking into a sucker punch on the queenside when you seemed on the verge of wrapping up on the kingside! But you do manage to salvage a draw in the final round!

This is by no means untypical, and many players continue to underperform for years without noticing that their main weaknesses are essentially fundamental psychological flaws. Ironically, when these same mistakes are explained in the annotations to a game we seem to have no problem appreciating them, but within a few hours we are quite capable of doing the very same. Because we understand each of our mistakes we have a 'reason' for them at the end of the game and we can explain them away as part of the game. This means there is no need to actually learn from these errors like we intend to from future games when it is appropriate. And so the cycle continues. The failure to realise that it is the factors that lead us astray that are crucial (rather than the mistakes themselves) is what holds us back, even serving to compound the problem.

'I don't seem to use my intelligence intelligently.'
Virginia Wade, 1977 Women's Wimbledon Champion

If we can learn to recognise the times and circumstances in a game when, for one reason or another, thought processes might let us down, then this will go a long way to improving results. In our everyday lives we are happy to become better acquainted with our weaknesses and habits as addressing them can improve the quality of life. Chess, like life, has the potential to be forever enriched by our own input.

The examples on these pages are designed to help us better recognise and appreciate how we – and our opponents – think and make decisions as a game progresses. From the beginning the aim of this book was to approach the subject of psychology in chess from a practical viewpoint. Finding oneself, being 'at one' with one's psyche and so on, sounds rather mystical. However, as far as chess is concerned, being attuned to our psychological strengths and weaknesses, to what effect various factors might have on the decision making process and on the ability to evaluate or calculate – these considerations are practical indeed. Psychology in general is a deep, deep subject in which to delve, but chess psychology as a practical tool can be approached in an almost methodical fashion and with a common-sense attitude.

Part One of this book deals with various off the board aspects of chess psychology and attitude, while the aim of Part Two is to investigate practical examples from a player's eye view. While I hope that the actual chess content will prove useful in helping you to better focus and analyse in future games, by trying to burrow into the protagonists' minds in order to concentrate on how and why this or that decision – good or bad – is made, my intention has been to lay the psychological foundations of a 'self-help' approach to the game. Learning from mistakes is one thing, but learning why they are made is another!

'I consider this defeat to be the mother of future victories.'
Antonio Oliveira, Portuguese football manager.

CHAPTER ONE

Psychological Factors

Inner Peace

'He that in his studies wholly applies himself to labour and exercise, and neglects meditation, loses his time; and he that only applies himself to meditation, and neglects labour and exercise, only wanders and loses himself.'
Confucius

There is more to life than chess. In fact life is part of chess, for nobody is capable of 'switching off' from everyday life before sitting down to play. Wives, mothers, brothers, work, school, planes, trains and automobiles, girlfriends, money, sleep, the common cold, husbands, football scores, back ache, weather, boyfriends, traffic lights, toothache, missing pens, the price of pens... the list of distractions that are detrimental to the cause is endless. Any number of factors, from the serious to the seemingly meaningless, can transform themselves into a considerable handicap even before you write your name down on your scoresheet. That's life! Chess can be difficult enough without life getting in the way of a complicated – or simple – variation. Of course some problems are so serious that you probably shouldn't be playing at all but, generally, distractions tend to be minor and it is likely that similar problems are experienced on both sides of the table.

A number of 'irritations' can be avoided, such as arriving late and – in most cases – losing time on your clock. The clock is an important part of the game and some players, unfortunately, allow just a few lost minutes to plague them for the rest of the game. In a tournament in Austria in the early 1990s I was sitting next to a game between two titled players in the penultimate round and my neighbour – let's call him Mr Always Early – who had the white pieces, and who would worry even at a few lost seconds, had arrived a minute or two late. The arbiter had started his clock as the opponent had not yet arrived and, aware (only vaguely, as it turned out) that with an absent opponent it was not necessary to actually play one's opening move on the board before pressing the clock, White simply set his opponent's clock running. Unfortunately to do this one is required to write down the move on the scoresheet, which Mr Always Early didn't get around to doing because he had been too concerned with not wasting any more time. Instead he took a stroll around the other top boards and gazed out of the window to the picture postcard scenery that surrounded the venue, outwardly pleased with the passing of every minute that his opponent's chair remained empty... His opponent – let's call him Mr Always Late – finally arrived, about forty-five minutes late. The two shook hands and, as Mr Always Late leaned over to check the spelling of his opponent's name on the scoresheet, he noticed that no move had been written down, so he called over the arbiter, pointed out the breach of the rules and asked for Mr Always Early to be penalised accordingly. Mr Always Early watched in horror as the arbiter picked up the clock and reversed the settings, leaving the new arrival with his full two hours and he with just over seventy minutes! Knowing the players concerned, I was not the only one who knew there and then that Black would win. He had succeeded in getting in a decisive psychological blow after arriving very late and before even writing his name down! In fact the writing ('0-1' in this case) was on the wall, as they say, before Black had sat down. Mr Always Early had become Mr Anxious.

I'm not sure what I would have done in Black's shoes as such gamesmanship can seem rather underhand (there was money at stake, I suppose), but there is more than one lesson to be learned here. Running short of time can be avoided but we are nevertheless 'justified' in experiencing stress when this happens, not least because the direct result is to reduce the accuracy of the decision making process.

Noisy Chess

Apart from life in general, more immediate factors can also adversely affect our demeanour or distract us in some way that has an adverse effect on the thought process. The most common problem is noise, whether this is chairs scraping on the floor, people talking, people walking, people coughing, traffic, hundreds of pieces being moved and taken and knocked over, the constant tapping of clocks being pressed, the sound of the seconds ticking away... For some players who have grown used to the soothing 'tick-tock' of standard chess clocks it is now the silence of digital clocks that they find distracting!

'Chess is a cure for headaches.'
John Maynard Keynes

Anyway, anxiety even at its most mild can be quite destructive. There has been some sports research to suggest that a certain level of anxiety can improve performance, which does sound feasible and might well be relevant to some extent in chess. If we approach a match or tournament game with too relaxed a manner there is a danger that our competitive 'edge' might be lacking – the aim of the game is to try to score points, after all! However, even this research suggests that once this anxiety level peaks, any subsequent increase then affects performance adversely. Because chess requires more clear thinking and pure concentration than conventional sports, it follows that anxiety is a handicap to chess players. When things aren't going well for us for some reason (we can easily be knocked off balance by our own form, of course – either before or during a game!) the very fact that we are conscious of having to 'knuckle down' and overcome our anxiety with a concerted effort can be detrimental in itself. What seems to come naturally when life is good – a mystical, all-seeing overview of each new situation, the ability to cut a direct path through a jungle of tactics, an appreciation of the long-term positional nuances etc. – suddenly requires a discernible, mechanical effort. This problem is particularly common among stronger players, whose better than average ability and understanding furnishes the luxury of a greater 'automatic' process. There is more to go wrong for stronger players; more labour-saving devices to stop working so smoothly. When under pressure the expert drifts closer to the level of the novice in terms of performance because he tries to contribute to a faltering automatic process with conscious control. The natural flowing nature of a player's skill is seriously damaged; the result of injecting the automatic process with conscious control breaks the fluidity of the skill. This has been termed 'deautomatisation' (Deikman, 1969). Organisers of so-called 'Super-GM' tournaments are able to provide their participants with excellent, distraction-free playing conditions in order to maximise the players' concentration and general well-being – at this level optimum conditions do indeed lead to optimum quality of games.

While it seems that the stronger the player the greater the adverse effect of the same level of anxiety, we all suffer from off-putting events of all proportions. We suffer more the more bad habits we have. For example the inner voice 'I go there, he goes there, I take that, he takes back...' approach as an analytical tool is not to be recommended even on a good day, but psychiatry rather than psychology will be required if these mantras need double-checking every time concentration is broken because someone scrapes a chair on the floor!

Another habit is to literally break down 'natural' or easy procedures to a fundamental level when we are worried that we are not thinking clearly. Not only do we doubt our ability to properly calculate short sequences or accurately assess what are normally simple positions, but we find ourselves triple checking how the pieces move, counting our pawns or gazing at the clock to check that nobody has stolen some of our precious time while we were busy adjusting all our pieces because we concentrate better when they are exactly in the centre of the squares! Incidentally, Gufeld wrote: 'It has been noted that when I am elated I place my pieces on the board accurately, but as soon as low spirits take over, "the pieces are almost tossed from square to square." I confess that in the past I have often suffered psychological breakdowns at tournaments.'

It is also possible that the extra effort prompted by anxiety might improve a player's performance, or at least re-establish the performance level through the extra effort. This compensatory effect does happen but, in the main, performance tends to be of a higher quality when stress levels are at a minimum. Moreover, with no half-time or other lull in the game, chess requires a certain (high) level of effort almost throughout, and any 'extra' would hardly be significant.

One Lump or Two?

Sometimes a change in diet can be helpful in addressing stress. Tea and coffee are by far the most popular drinks at a chess tournament, considered so important that their availability is even advertised on entry forms alongside the round times and so on. Yet after drinking large quantities of caffeine – it is not unusual to see players down several cups per game, sometimes several games per day! – we leave ourselves susceptible to feeling jittery and anxious. Even calm, non-coffee drinking players experience these two unfortunate states as a game progresses, so the army of coffee addicts at the average competition are clearly not helping themselves. Moreover, it is not unusual for players to take what might be a longish walk out of the playing hall and then queue for a not inconsiderable period just for another hot drink – this in itself is a typical cause of stress!

An 'unhealthy' diet is also believed to contribute to stress, although being too conscious of this might prompt us to address our diet in a rather drastic fashion, which can result in the adherence of the new and improved diet being so filled with tension that it causes stress!

Gamesmanship

Most unwelcome demands on our attention are accidental or – on the part of tournament or match organisers – unavoidable. However, the opponent is also capable of contributing to these inconveniences, unintentionally or otherwise (while chess might be considered a game of the fair its world has a large enough population to include in its ranks a number of unscrupulous types!).

'Nice guys finish last.'
Leo Durocher (1906-91), US baseball manager

'Last guys don't finish nice.'
Stanley Keeley, US academic

We have all been put off by an opponent at some stage of our chess career, most often when the time control (or the actual end of our allotted time) is fast approaching.

Blitzing

Probably the most 'popular' and successful way of breaking the rules (and experienced at all levels), this is when a player with over five minutes remaining on the clock tries to exploit his opponent's time-trouble by executing a series of moves without writing any down on the scoresheet. The most common example involves following up forced recaptures with another move or two (or three or four and so on if the victim allows the cheating to continue). As a player foolish enough to drift into time trouble regardless of how much time I am given at the start of the game, I am used to this sort of behaviour and I am not afraid to nip the dirty tricks in the bud immediately by demanding that my opponent abide by the rules and record my move, pointing out his attempt to an arbiter or, if an arbiter is not present, asking for one.

I once had the unpleasant experience of being repeatedly blitzed by a very well-known GM (I think he was once ranked number four in the world) who, not surprisingly, had used far less time than myself to reach a promising if rather complex position. His continued foul play and my accompanying complaints were ignored by the arbiter – who was, perhaps, too much in awe of my famous opponent's status in the chess world to notice he had failed to record a number of moves despite having well over an hour remaining on his clock– so I had to shout '*Stop Cheating*!', whereupon he pulled a rather unpleasant face and set about the 'inconvenience' of belatedly abiding by the rules. Of course he continued to try to win the game in my time shortage rather than use his extra time, superior position and vastly superior ability... and was punished with what must have been an embarrassing defeat (which, for me, was a sweet victory!). Unfortunately, with a limited number of arbiters already doing their utmost to police the playing hall during the latter stages of a session we occasionally have to stick up for ourselves – don't let your opponent cheat.

Other players prepared to venture beyond the boundaries of fair play in order to add a few points to their career tally might suddenly become clumsy during your time-trouble, knocking over a few pieces with a well placed sleeve or elbow (often when captures are taking place) yet nevertheless finding themselves pressing the clock before apologising and then kindly helping to properly place them – and all the time your seconds are slipping by! But the move is not complete – and therefore the clock cannot be pressed – until these knocked over pieces have been replaced.

The Clock as a Positional Tool

Knocking over the clock itself is a surprisingly popular trick, although this is a bit extreme. There are other unfair practices involving the clock. Picking it up to have a better look at the time situation is simply not allowed, while others use this fact to lean right over the board for a 'piece's eye view' – not only does this severely restrict your view of the board but it is also designed to delay your execution of your move by simply being in your way!

In my younger days – despite the fact that I first competed in chess events at the rather late age of ten, I was a time trouble veteran by the time I was a teenager – when I was smaller and quieter, it was not unusual to experience gamesmanship from older opponents. For example, in a weekend open in the north of England when I was about fourteen, my opponent thought he stood a better chance of exploiting my severe time shortage by moving the clock – which was already quite a way to my left, and I am right-handed – further and further away from my reach. At first this was a gradual process, arrested every few moves when I noticed my arm seemed to be getting shorter and had to bring it back to the edge of the board. But then our neighbours finished their game, which presented my opponent, now growing in confidence, with much more room for manoeuvre on his extended queenside. With my flag teetering on the brink he suddenly – quite purposefully, in fact – pushed the clock what must have been a record distance, and all this in front of a growing crowd! Not surprisingly, during this childish episode Mr Cheat's actual on the board play had deteriorated considerably, and mate was now inevitable, but before the game ended I managed to ask 'Would you prefer it if we put the clock in another room?' – an antidote that proved so satisfying that I have resorted to it a few times since (even in French).

Physical Chess?
Psychosomatic medicine deals with how the way we think can affect the functioning of the body, but what is important to chess players – at least it should be! – is how what we do with our bodies can affect how we think. Funnily enough I have always considered professional chess players to be rather lazy individuals. One of the attractions of the lifestyle for many players is being able to travel around the globe, stay in hotels, eat in restaurants and win money by playing (typically) just one game each day... all at the expense of sponsors (in an ideal world) and – hopefully – with not too much effort. Of course even talent should be accompanied by genuine hard work, so this description is a little simplistic, but it is safe to say that the average regular on the international open circuit does not lead a similar lifestyle to a professional tennis player in terms of their physical regime! However, in the modern game, where adjournments are no longer available and the time limits even at the highest echelons of international practice are getting faster and faster, any chess player serious enough to want to improve should really be addressing the fitness issue.

Even as a child I was aware of the *healthy body, healthy mind* advice, but many chess players seem not too keen on categorising chess as a sport if this means giving credence to its physical aspect. Perhaps this attitude is a deliberate distinction that allows a chess player who lacks interest in or does not excel at conventionally physical sports to point out he or she still possesses a talent, but in another field ('she's a good swimmer, but I am a strong chess player'). Or do chess players feel that their game lacks the recognition it deserves, and so downplay the argument about whether chess should be 'elevated' to sport status? Personally, I believe that chess is as much a sport as a number of other competitive games that are considered by all to fall into this category, while some 'experts' prefer to call it an art, others a science and so on. Karpov summed it up perfectly with the opinion: 'Chess is everything – art, science and sport.' I write these lines, of course, sitting comfortably in my easy chair, with my feet up and my favourite music playing in the background! Needless to say, I endeavour to make sure that an energy drink is always within reach...

As far as the extent of the possible effect of physical activity on psychological well-being is concerned, recent research suggests that there is a positive association between the two, although which way round is not clear – does feeling upbeat prompt us to go out for a jog, or do we experience improved mental well-being after performing thirty sit-ups? An interesting subject, but it is logical to assume that by remaining healthy we at least maintain a desirable psychological state that might well facilitate a level of mental agility that augurs well for our chess career. Physical inactivity, conversely, is associated with more negative emotions.

'Physical fitness is not only one of the most important keys to a healthy body, it is the basis of dynamic and creative intellectual activity. The relationship between the soundness of the body and the activities of the mind is subtle and complex. Much is not yet understood. But we do know what the Greeks knew: that intelligence and skill can only function at the peak of their capacity when the body is healthy and strong; that hardy spirits and tough minds usually inhabit sound gods.'
John F. Kennedy

Kasparov might be greying at the temples but he still exudes an almost buzzing energy, and throughout his dazzling career he has made a point of devoting a good part of his chess preparation to achieving a level of physical fitness on a par with conventional athletes. In recent years the young pretenders have followed his example, and a fitness regime is now readily accepted as a necessary part of a serious player's all-round training.

Sleep

We don't all sleep for the same amount of time each night, and scientific research cannot determine exactly how many hours an individual needs in order to function well but, nevertheless, sleeping in itself is clearly going to affect our ability to perform the many tasks we face during everyday life. Thinking is one of these, and when our thought processes need to be channelled specifically into chess it is not possible to be at our best if thoughts of a nice, pleasant rest invade our detailed calculations of a sequence of sacrifices or interrupt an evaluation of a complex of potentially weak pawns at the end of a series of exchanges. Experts involved in any sport warn against a lack of sleep, while it is not unusual for chess trainers to recommend an extra period of rest or relaxation before a game. For instance at international tournaments my good friend James Howell (GM) used to have a short nap of thirty minutes or so about an hour before the game. And he would always make sure to get a good night's sleep. Apart from his talent and other factors, I am sure that this routine helped.

For most people between seven or eight hours each night is about right, some might need considerably more and others very little. Unfortunately, what we should do and what we do do are often different and, in the main, less rather than more sleep is the usual result. One of the attractions of chess is its social life, and whether we're taking a break from everyday life to play in a two day competition, a weekend of national league matches or a nine day international tournament it is only natural to want to relax with friends and other players in the evening after a taxing day of mental combat. There are also those for whom there is no reminder from an inner clock that it is time for bed. Nevertheless, just as we need to make an effort away from the board in terms of preparation and learning, as well as the obvious effort during a game, it is worth trying to guarantee at least a certain amount of time for sleep. Not only will you feel (literally) wide awake and more alert, but this addition to your armoury also serves as a confidence booster.

Lack of Sleep

At a recent National Chess League weekend I ended a very busy day of hours of travel, captain's duties, playing in the match itself, the journey to the team's hotel, a (too late) meal and catching up on life with my friends not by doing the sensible thing and going straight to bed but... staying awake so that I could watch the fortunes and otherwise of Michael Schumacher and his rivals in the Australian Grand Prix, 'live' on television! By the time I had finished watching the race it was almost time to take a much needed revitalising shower and nip downstairs for breakfast. I must admit that I did feel rather guilty (both in terms of my own prospects and those of my team), but why break what is a – I admit, rather unprofessional – habit of a lifetime? The twist to this story, of course, would be that after sitting down on the top board of the fixture (Black against a titled player, just to make life that bit more difficult) I played an excellent game and came away with the full point after four hours of chess mastery. In fact that is not too far from what did actually happen, the only difference being that after an exciting game in which I sacrificed two exchanges(!) and emerged with a winning ending... I lost on time on the 39th move! Whoops.

Habit of a lifetime, I said. A long time ago, during my days as a youngster who thought that sleep was a bit of an inconvenience, my quest for the IM title took me to Benidorm – not an obvious place for an international chess tournament, you're probably thinking, and you'd be right. I had managed to somehow put together a week of good results and needed only a draw against any FIDE rated player in the ninth and final round to add an IM norm to my collection. Under these circumstances, and with the game starting at 8am, it would not be unreasonable to make sure I had a good night's sleep, thus breaking my 'holiday' routine for the previous seven or eight nights. Alas, in my wisdom I 'calculated' that to alter my rhythm so drastically could only be detrimental, whereas relaxing throughout the night and not going to bed at all would even allow me to return to base at around 7am, shower and breakfast before the game in what promised to be a natural flowing preparation. A quick draw offer with the white pieces against a lower rated player would do the trick, after which I could sleep (if required). The plan went well until just before the round started when, after a hearty breakfast, I saw that I had been paired with a strong IM (soon after a strong GM) from Argentina. After a dozen or so moves of a game that I began with 1 ♘f3 2 g3 3 ♗g2 4 0-0 I crossed my fingers and offered a draw, but he did not even acknowledge my offer and sank into a deep, deep think. I started to walk around and became increasingly concerned with each passing minute, hoping that he would look up with a smile and accept and wishing that I had been sensible enough to sleep before such an important game – I was there, after all, to play well, not holiday. After more than forty minutes, I saw him make his move and, with a horrible, nervous feeling inside I made my way back to the board, suddenly physically exhausted, psychologically beaten and totally unprepared – in every way – to fight for my much needed draw against a stronger player. As I sat down and began to write down his move, my opponent wearily leaned across the board and said in a hoarse voice: 'I offer a draw'... As I grabbed his hand and accepted at such a speed that would prevent him from forgetting what he'd just said, I told him that I had also offered three quarters of an hour earlier, and he said that hadn't noticed – he was too tired after being out all night and only just managed to get to the hotel in time. In case you're wondering, I made more than enough norms for the IM title, which did not hinge on this fortuitous episode. But the fact remains that I was nearly punished for my stupidity, and I did learn a lot from this experience. Many years later I was wrong to watch the Grand Prix, but in general I have practised what I preach. Sleep is an important part of a chess player's preparation, and neglecting this area of your game can have implications as serious as not bothering to double-check for blunders during your deliberations at the board – something which is far more likely to happen, of course, if you don't get a good night's sleep! Furthermore, tests have shown that a lack of sleep can lead to weariness, poor concentration, a decline in creativity and a slowing down in reaction time – all very relevant for us chess players!

'I have won many games that have not made me happy; and when I lose, I am also not happy. My friends ask 'so when are you happy?' That's the way chess is; you are happy only rarely; the rest is grief.'
GM Ljubomir Ljubojevic (*Inside Chess*, 1993)

What is my Motivation?

'The need for achievement is a stable, learned characteristic in which satisfaction is obtained by striving for and attaining a level of excellence.'
McClelland, Atkinson, Clark & Lowell, 1953

I remember messing up a couple of winning positions against stronger players as a promising junior and not being satisfied by the praise I received for a good tournament result because I knew I could – indeed should! – have won the event. My grief was compounded when someone tried to reassure me with the fact that I had had an 'enjoyable' week. What was he talking about? The 'it's the taking part that counts' theory was alien to me. I had a chance of (relative) glory and threw it away.

Today, on the other hand, having for one reason or another failed to fulfil my initial promise in some respects (my one GM performance is a decade or so old), it is a number of years since I felt even a fraction of the ambition and motivation I experienced in my late teens and early twenties. Then I used to call myself a HYP chess player – a Hungry Young Professional. Now, at 35, I am married, with bills to pay, things to see and do, interests that have absolutely nothing to do with chess and for which I had little time for in my younger days, and a wonderfully entertaining 15-month-old daughter. Consequently the chess part of my life nowadays consists almost exclusively of writing and editing (and coaching). There is little time for playing and, quite frankly, I don't care any more. But that is not to say that I no longer enjoy playing chess. This was the case in the mid to late 1990s, when habit led me to continue playing, with no desire, no ambition, no fun and in an increasingly number-crunching, database oriented environment that was definitely not conducive to the old-fashioned minimal/no (usually 'no') preparation approach. Needless to say my play suffered considerably.

'In my opinion, the ability to enjoy the game is one of the main factors that sustain one's motivation level.'
GM Boris Gelfand (*Schahmat*, 1999)

These days, playing serious chess is so far down my list of priorities that it has assumed a casual – even relaxation – status, to such an extent that I am looking forward to diving once again into the ocean that is international competition. Preparing – once I get around to it – might well prove to be an enjoyable exercise. Sitting down to play a nine round international will have a 'buzz' for me, and the time and effort the tournament will take from my everyday life will illicit in me an albeit temporary professional attitude. And herein lies the beauty of chess – it can offer so much to so many.

'Winning isn't everything, but making the effort is.'
Vince Lombardi (1913-70), American football coach

Different people play for different reasons, and even for an individual devotee these reasons can change, back and forth, over the years, during which a gradual improvement will be dotted with good, bad and indifferent periods. My story, thus far, is by no means untypical, with varying degrees of ambition, commitment, enjoyment and (lack of) success. After twenty-five years I am still interested. The motivation is still there.

'Winning isn't everything, but wanting to is.'
Arnold Palmer, US golfer

As much as we do enjoy chess, and as much as we like to think that results are not *that* important, at the end of a game there are, invariably, only two possible outcomes: one player wins while the other loses, or the point is shared (if both players have been naughty, perhaps, they could be in for a double default). These points are awarded because chess is a competitive game. Consequently, before we sit down to play, it would be rather strange not to approach the game with at least some kind of competitive spirit, preferably a will to win.

'You have to expect things of yourself before you can do them.'
Michael Jordan, US basketball player

Research (McClelland, 1961; Atkinson, 1957) into motivation in sport has generally found that a characteristic of high achievers is that they strive for success and yet do not fear failure. Such people tend to be drawn towards competition and difficult but realisable challenges.

'Winning doesn't really matter as long as you win.'
Vinnie Jones

Lower achievers, on the other hand, typically avoid personal challenges by playing weaker opposition or (worse) by setting goals that are realistically beyond reach and therefore not too demanding or threatening. In British chess there are many players who would be better described as under-achievers, as they are able to both limit their opposition to below a specific level but also enjoy success as winners. As a coach at international level for both juniors (numerous world championships) and adults (Olympiads and tournaments) it is interesting that my overseas counterparts have suggested that the almost unique British weekend congress set-up of splitting up the players into several sections according to (official) playing strength – typically, Opens, Majors, Intermediate, Minor, Novice and Junior tournaments! – is detrimental to the improvement of young players (or any players, for that matter). While players of all strengths across the Channel participate alongside others with much higher ratings, as well as IMs and GMs, in one large section, in Britain we are offered the 'protection' of not having to face anyone over a certain grading or rating bracket. Such a restrictive attitude to competition might well produce literally hundreds of 'winners' across the country every weekend but, in the long term, as far as juniors or would-be improvers are concerned, this simply holds us back. Surely, if we invest time and money turning up to play in tournaments, then an improvement of results through actual improvement in strength is our goal, and the surest way to do this is by taking on stronger opposition. 'But it is easier to beat weaker players' is an unfortunately common response. True, but over time wins will come against stronger players, more regularly, and then even stronger victims, and so on. We never stop learning, and we never stop improving, but both will be severely hampered if we limit our ambition so drastically, and in so doing destroy any real motivation, by refusing to acknowledge our ever expanding sphere of potential. Nevertheless, the ego is a strange animal, and because motivation is linked to effort, performance, rewards and – ultimately – satisfaction, these factors mean different things to different people. Ironically, an amateur player in France, for example, who enjoys chess, will participate in an open-to-all tournament and typically win a few games, draw a few and lose a few, meeting some strong opposition – perhaps a well-known GM – along the way and occasionally winning a very decent prize for the best performance in his rating category. He or she will have benefited in terms of effort, performance, rewards and satisfaction; but the British 'everyman' system of multi-section congresses runs the risk of creating a nation of chess 'fans' for whom the opportunity to play the likes of Julian Hodgson, Mark Hebden, Keith Arkell and a host of other top players is – to put it mildly – frowned upon. It is difficult to imagine the same player, who might play 'fun' football on alternate weekends, turning down an invitation to face David Beckham or Michael Owen, or a golf enthusiast showing absolutely no interest whatsoever if Tiger Woods was getting ready to tee off alongside!

'Success is important but defeats are valuable.'
C.M.Jones, British journalist

A positive attitude does not preclude the acknowledgement that, somewhere along the line, we are going to lose a game! That is simply a fact of life, from absolute beginner to world champion. Given that this is going to happen we should aim high in all aspects of competition. Adopting a negative, blinkered approach seems at best to succeed in furnishing artificial rewards and false satisfaction, while effort and performance continue to be neglected. The words 'eggs' and 'omelette' once again come into play – if you're bothering to turn up, you might as well (if only occasionally) play stronger opposition. Once we have established what we want from chess (enjoyment, experience, improvement, relative success...) the journey ahead will be all the more satisfying.

We can label the four main attributive elements in sport as follows: ability, effort, task and luck. As far as we are concerned, an internal factor such as ability plays a far greater role than luck (external) compared with football or golf, for example. Consequently self-reliance is paramount to a chess player – even in a team event – for the end result is in a very large part dependent on our own, exclusive qualities.

Our competence is in the spotlight from the moment the seconds begin to count down, so if we have insufficient faith in our abilities every game will be difficult. A healthy dose of confidence and motivation, then, is a good foundation, and there is every justification in adopting such an attitude. Research by Harter (1981) suggests that perceptions of competence will influence both the initiation of participation and, subsequently, continued participation. Additionally, intrinsic motivation tends to lead to us sticking with the game and to the responsibilities we undertake to get the most out if. Without motivation, effort will suffer, as will performance, which in turn will limit satisfaction. And if satisfaction is lacking, so will motivation, both diminishing until the cycle ends.

Memory

'Personally, I never clutter up my memory with facts I can easily find in an encyclopaedia.'
Albert Einstein

Memory is the process by which we encode, store and retrieve information. It follows that a certain level of appreciation of how the memory works is of paramount importance to chess players.

Memories... in the Corner of my Mind

If only we could remember every move that we have played, seen being played, read in books and whizzed through on a computer database – that would be most impressive and incredibly useful (allied with factors such as skill, understanding etc.). In reality, of course, not only do we have problems assimilating all the necessary information when studying the intricacies of just one specific opening variation – which, in itself, requires considerable concentration and clear thinking if sequences of moves and relevant points are going to be stored – but it is also not unusual to forget a good deal of recent preparation. If we know what our opponent plays we can be tempted – often at the prompting of friends and team mates – into 'learning' a completely new line or system, with the intention of trying out a new idea or in the hope of catching out the opponent with a 'trap' and so on. Such an approach is foolhardy anyway, but a common result is the embarrassing situation in which, somewhere along the way, we forget a key move or idea, finding ourselves looking at an almost alien position which, don't forget, is part of the opponent's repertoire! Memory is by no means everything in chess, being just one of a number of factors, but it helps to be aware of our strengths and weaknesses in this respect, and of how our memory works.

Chunks

The short-term memory is a severely limited capacity store, and it is generally considered that we store information for fifteen to twenty-five seconds. The specific amount of information that can be held in short-term memory has been identified as seven items, or 'chunks' of information, a chunk being a meaningful grouping of stimuli that can be stored as a unit in our short-term memory. For example, give yourself ten seconds to take in the following collection of letters:

M D A P F C I

This is a rather simple and easy task, since there are only seven letters, each of which represents a chunk of information, and can be readily stored in the short-term memory. Now try the following, much longer list, this time for thirty seconds:

A T P F B I M T V B B C C B S A B C R I P

How did you do this time? Not too well, perhaps, given that there are now as many as twenty-one separate letters, simply too many chunks to recall after just one attempt. However, let's have a go at the same list of letters but, this time, I will present them in a different way:

ATP FBI MTV BBC CBS ABC RIP

Well done (I hope). While there are still twenty-one letters the task of storing them is made much simpler now because they have been grouped together into only seven chunks.

These groups can be of varying sizes and categories, and specific to our personal experience. Therefore an experienced chess player might have more success recalling a new, albeit familiar, orthodox chess position made up of twenty-five pieces than, for example, recognising the faces of six strangers on a photograph.

Although it is possible to remember around seven even complex sets of information that are stored in the short-term memory, this information cannot remain there for very long. Thus in order to benefit from study sessions, whether this involves reading books or playing through games on a database, we need to appreciate how best to transfer important information from its temporary home to the more permanent and potentially useful refuge of the long-term memory.

Practice Makes Perfect
No it doesn't, but it is worth approaching any kind of chess work with such an attitude. In order to remember a new telephone number we might repeat it several (many) times, keeping it well placed in the short-term memory with the hope of establishing it in the long-term memory. The transfer of material from short-term to long-term memory through repetition is known as rehearsal. Whether the transfer is made seems to depend to some extent on what kind of rehearsal is being carried out. For example if we also use the new telephone number as soon as we have

stored it, other information is likely to replace the number as soon as we have finished dialling, and there is a chance it will be forgotten through this interference.

If we are to benefit from experience and learning in chess we need to make maximum use of our memory, and this means using a process known as elaborate rehearsal. This occurs when the material is considered and organised in some sort of ordered fashion. By engineering a logical framework from the information in front of us we are then able to store ideas, themes, techniques, theoretical developments and so on in a way that facilitates our recalling them when the appropriate time comes. This is why trying to remember only the actual moves of variations in openings and defences rather than the reasoning behind them and their various positional, structural, tactical and general thematic implications is simply not good enough. Not only are we anyway less likely to actually store these lines but, even if we succeed, we will experience difficulties finding the essence of this or that situation as the game progresses. After the game, of course, it is a good idea to play through it – ideally with the opponent – in order to better recall any important thoughts and possibilities, which can be written down, studied until fully appreciated and then put in storage.

Super Storage

Information that finds its way from short-term to long-term memory enters an enormous storehouse that is of almost unlimited capacity. The more we understand what we take in, the more logical our internal filing system and, in turn, the easier it becomes to retrieve the most relevant information.

The 'pattern recognition' that is often associated with stronger players is a rather simplistic description of their ability to home in on only the most relevant factors in a given position. In fact a highly ranked GM seems to have the facility of 'theme' or 'strategy' recognition, for example. To appreciate the vastness of a top player's Chess Storehouse, imagine a section exclusively devoted to the relationship between a rook and bishop team versus rook and knight in endings with pawns on both flanks, or another department featuring only opening situations in which White has pawns on a2, b2, d4, f2, g2, h2, Black on a7, b7, e6, f7, g7, h7, Black's light-squared bishop still on c8 and with a pair of knights already exchanged! How often have you seen a strong player analysing a game or opening and suggesting a move (or dismissing one) on the grounds that 'in this kind of position White should be doing this' or 'Black must avoid trading dark-squared bishops with this structure' etc? These specific categories are typical of what can be found in a strong player's armoury, and they get there through hard work.

Experience is more than just playing lots of games – obviously if we were to play throughout the year in marathon theme tournaments in which, for example, every game had to start 1 e4 e6 2 d4 d5 3 ♘d2, then even without preparation or a single post mortem we would eventually store information about pawn chains (after 3...♘f6 4 e5 ♘fd7 5 f4 c5 6 c3 etc.) and IQP positions (after 3...c5 4 exd5 exd5 and an eventual dxc5 or ...cxd4 etc.) and so on, the repetition being enough (it would make sense and be far more rewarding to actually study, of course). Implicit memory begins to kick in after a large amount of games, the sheer volume of related positions planting memories of which we are not consciously aware but which can improve subsequent performance. In reality, however, it is our own responsibility to make sure to follow the process of elaborate rehearsal and to broaden our horizons as much as possible, learning by understanding along the way. Only then can we be the proud curators of an impressive and very useful mental chess collection. Explicit memory – the intentional or conscious recollection of information – is an incredibly useful tool. If we have the time, by studying and rehearsing past the point of initial mastery, we can further improve our recall – this process is called *overlearning*. Every now and then we should review material, whether this is opening theory, endgame technique, various middlegame strategies etc. In this way we reach an optimum level of overlearning.

De Groot (1966) investigated the possibility that GMs have far more positions stored in the long-term memory than weaker players. Positions from actual games were presented to GMs and lesser players for a period of only five seconds, after which the players were asked to reconstruct the positions. The GMs managed a success rate of 91%, while the second group were correct only 41% of the time. The next test, on the other hand, concerned only positions where the pieces were arranged randomly, and this time the performance of the two groups in reconstructing was the same. This would suggest that stronger players can relate positions to stored knowledge (previous games), and this contributes to the level of performance.

Simon and Gilmartin concentrated on this subject of storage in 1973 when they developed two versions of a computer model known as the Memory-Aided Pattern Perceiver (MAPP). One version had access to 1114 stored chess patterns, the other only 894, and the former was better at reconstructing positions. After comparing the performance of MAPP and master level chess players at reconstructing positions Simon and Gilmartin estimated that masters probably have between 10,000 and 100,000 chess patterns stored in long-term memory. Obviously the difficulty of the measurement of such storage is reflected in these figures, but it would not be surprising for an experienced GM, for example, to accumulate a vast number of stored positions during the course of a career spanning several decades.

Incidentally, a major problem with 'automatically' remembering only the moves of, for example, the main line of the Exchange Variation of the Ruy Lopez – as a regular part of an opening repertoire rather than a one-off, cramming session just before a game – is the 'tip-of-the-tongue' phenomenon. This is when we have difficulty recalling information that we know we know, and is usually experienced when we have not faced a particular line for a while and have at best an insufficient knowledge of its secrets. A more detailed long-term memory, one that features relevant material other than just the moves themselves, has far more chance of being retrieved thanks to what many psychologists call *associative models*. This is a technique of recalling information by thinking about related information. For example, if we have learned that at some point in a particular line Black should seek to push the b-pawn, relocate the king's knight and engineer a trade of queens, and why these are part of Black's strategy, then these clues help us log on to the theoretical sequences we are looking for. It is logical that increasing the number of stimuli provides us with more choice of information and serves to facilitate the retrieval process, and the more distinctive the stimulus the more readily it is recalled (a line featuring a destructive queen sacrifice is easier to remember than one in which not a great deal happens).

Food and Drink

The chemical nature of memory is such that everyday factors can interfere with the physiology of memory consolidation. Not surprisingly, certain kinds of food might be associated with memory. For example, recent research suggests that even some-thing like a tall glass of lemonade may serve to aid the memory. Experiments have shown that an increase in the level of glucose in the blood can produce an im-provement in performance in memory, although energy drinks, high in glucose, are fairly popular anyway among some players. I have noticed GM Chris Ward turn up for games with such a drink despite the fact that the cheerful chappie seems bubbly enough without one.

Alcohol acts as a 'sedative' of the central nervous system, slowing down communication between nerve cells. Consequently, when a person is under the influence of alcohol, temporary interference occurs in the consolidation of memo-ries. Wine and chess don't mix.

Thinking

We take in such a vast amount of information, across a fantastic range of subjects, that we cannot expect to have chess themes, strategies and winning ideas readily available, to simply pluck from the memory with no effort and then transfer to the chess board. Somewhere along the line a certain amount of thinking is required. And the more we have actually thought about chess in the past, the easier this should be – and the more information will have been logically stored in our own private databases. 'Stored' does not necessarily mean remembered, so we have to get used to thinking, to analysing, in order to make the most of our experience.

Back in 1966 a study by De Groot asked GMs and untitled players to express their thoughts when contemplating their moves. Despite the fact that the GMs produced superior moves they did not consider more alternatives than the other players, and nor did they analyse the possibilities in greater detail. However, later research (Holding, 1989) suggested that stronger players tend to think further ahead than weaker players.

Remember that there is a lot more to being a strong player than simply adding as many positions as possible to the mental database, just as devoting every waking minute to building the world's greatest vocabulary will not win you the Nobel Prize for literature! Tests by Holding and Reynolds (1982), which supported De Groot's work that found no difference between stronger and weaker players in the ability to reconstruct random positions, went on to find that the stronger players succeeded, in fact, in finding superior moves to weaker players in these random positions. This indicates that stronger players possess superior skills in addition to their greater knowledge of positions. These superior skills might well manifest themselves to some degree in the master's greater ability to actually learn and store important information, over an incredibly wide range of subjects and within a logical framework. Fortunately, everyone is capable of improvement, and a good place to start is by addressing how we work at the game away from the board – what we analyse, how we analyse, how we maximise our understanding of key themes and, ultimately, how we come to store all this useful material.

CHAPTER TWO

Practical Examples

Exploiting an Advantage

How good is a good position? Which is better, a positional superiority that could make life difficult for the opponent but which holds no immediate advantage, or extra material in potentially inconvenient circumstances, when the opponent might have 'extra' activity? There is no correct answer, of course, and each situation should be judged on its merits but, when human nature kicks in, we tend to put our faith in the latter scenario. We teach children and absolute beginners that there is more to winning a game of chess than checkmate. Taking this simple logic further (but not too far), there is certainly a lot more to most games than the goal of winning material. Yet as soon as such a prospect reveals itself we tend to forget about the deeper concepts we have taken the trouble of considering thus far – and around which the game could well continue to revolve – and instead head straight for the booty. We have a feeling that we should keep up the good work as good positions have the habit of playing themselves but,

nevertheless, inherent in such a policy is an element of doubt, that maintaining an albeit favourable tension involves some kind of risk. What if we have overestimated our hold on the game? What if our positional pluses are illusory and we will come to regret not going down the route that guarantees, for example, netting a pawn? Patiently sitting on our advantage both lacks the attraction of instant reward and keeps alive the opponent's prospects of generating significant counterplay or even turning the tables in his favour. Even worse – and herein we find a key factor – is the theory that while the situation remains more complex, while more hard work is required to keep us in the driving seat, the possibility of making a mistake (particularly a serious one) is higher than would be the case in a simpler position, which usually results after a (forcing) series of exchanges. It is this fear, this shortage of confidence, which tends to be the main contributor in determining which course to take when we are confronted with important questions.

The reason why we so often take the

'easy' route is best appreciated when we look back to poor streaks of form when, afraid to lose again or let another well played game slip away, we take the opportunity to simplify to advantage with scant consideration of alternatives. However, when results are good and confidence is high we are happy to retain the tension if we feel that our pressure or positional advantage puts the opponent under uncomfortable pressure. Then, ironically, the idea of 'spoiling' the picture in front of us for the win of a mere pawn – at the cost of renewed hope for the opponent – seems quite silly! Unfortunately, in terms of the desired, successful 'mind over matter' approach to chess, it is the ability to evaluate the actual and practical factors hidden in future positions that we need to nurture. Of course this is easier said than done, which is why we so often find ourselves voluntarily – indeed, quite forcefully – steering a game into territory in which there is an ostensibly clear-cut plus only to see the implications of affording the opponent some freedom and, usually, unwelcome activity result in improving his chances. It is interesting that there is such a fine line between right and wrong decisions in these situations, for hastily relinquishing collective advantages does tend to happen when the same plan could be executed under more favourable circumstances in the near future. Here is an example from international practice:

Vallejo Pons-I.Sokolov
Mondariz 2001

How would you assess this position?

With which side do you feel most comfortable? Well, Black has the bishop pair while White has more space and more influence in the centre. The youngster seeks to exploit both these advantages.

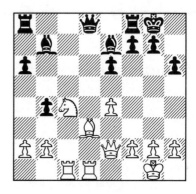

White to move

21 e5

Increasing White's territorial supremacy, preparing to rid Black of the bishop pair and throwing in the threat of ♗h7+ for good measure – not a difficult move to find.

21...♕b8 22 ♗e4 ♗xe4 23 ♕xe4

With White's advantages (superior minor piece, more space, better posted, more active forces, unchallenged command of the light squares) still intact and Black's gone, White stands better. Already we are quite happy to place ourselves in White's shoes. Black, on the other hand, has seen significant potential in his stock decline with the exchange of bishops. Understandably, then, White's confidence should be riding high at this point.

23...♗g5 24 ♖c2 ♖d8 25 ♖xd8+ ♕xd8 26 ♘d6 ♖b8 27 ♕f3

An instructive case of a dual-purpose, offensive/defensive move. White prevents ...b4-b3 while hitting f7. Notice how, over the next few moves, White accentuates his command of the situation.

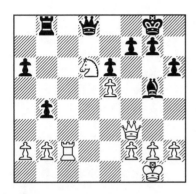

27...♕d7 28 g3

28 ♖c4 also favours White, e.g. 28...f6 29 h4 fxe5 30 hxg5 ♕xd6 31 gxh6.

28...♖f8

Coming to the aid of f7 leaves the queenside pawns looking even more vulnerable, which explains White's next.

29 ♕c6 ♕a7 30 ♖c4

Another nice move, using the rook to both attack b4 and keep the enemy queen out of d4. White's confidence in his pluses has resulted in him dominating, with the queen and rook adding weight to the knight's contribution. Of course, with Black now quite passive, life is even easier for White, who should be looking to remain in control.

30...a5 31 ♔g2 ♖d8 32 h4

Reminding Black who is in charge. With potential targets in the shape of Black's queenside pawns and advanced, powerful pieces taking care of the centre White turns the screw by expanding on the kingside.

32...♗e7 33 ♘c8 ♕d7

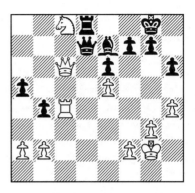

There is no disputing White's influence on the light squares here, but it is the general bind and Black's shortage of both space and decent moves that make up the key factor. Consequently White should continue in the fashion that has served him so well thus far. However, as is so often the case when we have the opponent struggling, White now makes the mistake of releasing the tension in order to earn himself a material gain.

34 ♕xd7?!

Premature. White's eagerness to trade his dominating pieces to win a pawn is understandable and, indeed, quite typical. Moreover, such a reaction to the prospect of steering the game apparently 'closer to victory' is so natural that it is by no means unusual to see such an error of judgement even in top level chess. In this particular case it is worth noting White's relative inexperience. Perhaps older, more patient players would have opted instead for the more appropriate, stronger 34 h5!, which furthers the cause on the light squares and 'fixes' two more pawns on the same colour complex as the bishop. There is also the matter of Black – for whom life has been growing increasingly difficult since we joined the game – having to find a decent move! We can conclude that maintaining the pressure with h4-h5 serves to accentuate White's supremacy and, in doing so, adds to Black's defensive burden – a success both on the board and psychologically. Tsesarsky gives the following variation as an example of how the game could continue: 34...♗f8 35 ♕xd7 ♖xd7 36 ♘b6 ♖d2 37 ♖c8 f6 38 ♔f3 fxe5 39 ♔e3 ♖d6 40 ♘c4 ♖d5 41 ♔e4

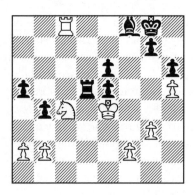

White has a clear advantage. Note that trading White's impressive queen in this fashion has not diminished the domination enough to alleviate Black's defensive problems, allowing White to remain in the driving seat well into the ending.

34...♖xd7

Instead the game continued:

35 ♘xe7+ ♖xe7 36 ♖c8+?!

Part of the new and rather simplistic plan to round up the a5-pawn. A better winning try is 36 ♖c5, e.g. 36...♖a7 (36...♖d7 37 ♖xa5 ♖d2 38 b3) 37 a4! bxa3 38 bxa3 a4 39 h5 when White retains his hold on what is left of the position and Black is once again under pressure to hold.

36...♔h7 37 ♖a8 b3!

Perhaps White missed this cheeky advance which, despite the points score, reverses roles and serves to reduce White to passivity.

38 ♖xa5

After 38 axb3 ♖b7 39 ♖xa5 ♖xb3 40 ♖a2 ♔g6 41 g4 h5! Black has considerable activity, while 38 a3 ♖d7 39 ♖xa5 ♖d2 is completely level.

38...bxa2 39 ♖xa2 ♖b7

While it is quite possible that White had failed to spot – or fully appreciate the implications of – Black's pawn sacrifice with ...b4-b3, the course of the game has nonetheless demonstrated that there is an element of the unknown in what might seem to be forcing sequences. Checking for blunders and obvious (unwelcome) compensation for the opponent is difficult enough, without having to then evaluate accurately the resulting positions after a series of exchanges, and this is how the defender tends to emerge with something or other. We are often sufficiently satisfied that we can force the win of, for example, a 'safe' pawn, content to leave the work on the next phase of the game until the smoke has cleared. Unfortunately by then it might be too late, as Vallejo Pons now discovers. White's rook could not be more poorly placed, sitting next to the passed pawn rather than behind it. From b7, on the other hand, Black's rook enjoys considerable influence.

40 ♔f3 ♔g6 41 ♔e4 h5 42 f4 ♖b3 43 ♖a3 ½-½

Not only did White's change of direction to the extra pawn ending fail to deliver, but the turnaround was quite rapid, with Black's prospects improving almost immediately after White had removed the target.

Familiarity Breeds Success

There is no denying these days that in order to achieve any kind of improvement in our results we must put together a decent openings repertoire. Being in a healthy psychological state before we sit down to begin a game is of paramount importance, and the reassuring feeling of being armour-plated with a wealth of theoretical knowledge is a terrific confidence-booster. However, the study of opening theory concerns far more than blindly remembering sequences of moves and assessments. Rather it is an understanding of key positional, tactical and strategic issues that should be nurtured, and this is best addressed by becoming acquainted with ideas and themes that are present during the middlegame phase. Diving beneath the surface that is the opening stage and plunging deeper into the ostensibly murky waters of the middlegame – and yet further to the ending – is the only way. Failure to do so will lead to lost opportunities when the

game really gets going. Take a look at the following position, arising from the Sicilian Sveshnikov:

Wolter-Von Herman
German Championship 2001

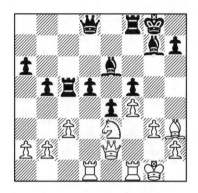

Black to move

How would you assess this situation? Here is a plausible sounding evaluation: Black has the two bishops, reasonably active forces and a territorial supremacy spearheaded by the well protected passed e4-pawn. But Black also has three pawn islands (compared with two for White), the middle cluster providing White with targets in the shape of the backward pawns on f5 and d5. With this in mind White's knight is superbly posted on e3, with both pawns in its sights, and from where it can jump to c2 in order to accentuate White's control of the d4-square (ownership of the square in front of a backward pawn tends to confer an advantage). Additionally the rook furthers this cause, and it is always nice to have a rook on the same file as the enemy queen. Meanwhile White's bishop hits f5 and keeps alive the possibility – albeit not without risk – of breaking with g3-g4 etc. If Black rids himself of the problem pawn with ...d5-d4 he walks into a pin on the d-file (after the trade on d4) and the weakness remains on f5. It seems fair to say that White has his opponent under control...

Now let us put the position to one side for a moment and consider the state of play in the diagram below:

Black to move

So, a very similar situation from the same variation. What do we think of this one? Well, again Black has the same three pawn islands, and White the very same structure. Here too White has concentrated on his opponent's backward d-pawn, this time actually occupying the square in front of it. Further undermining of Black's centre has taken place with f2-f4, fixing the f5-pawn, and White's extra knight is poised to make its presence felt on e3. We appear to have another case of Black's bishops and would-be menacing forces being kept at bay by White, whose positional lead is evident. Indeed these are generally convincing arguments that White stands comfortably better in these

closely related positions...

However, in Tseshkovsky-Kharlov, Vladivostok 1990 Black played 20...b4!, and White's grip on the centre disappeared after 21 cxb4 (the alternative to surrendering the d4-square is to accept an isolated c3-pawn after ...bxc3) 21...axb4 22 ♘cxb4 ♘xb4 23 ♘xb4 e4

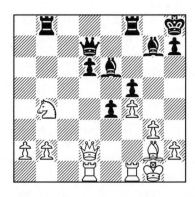

Exploiting the tactic 24 ♕xd6 ♕xd6 25 ♖xd6 ♗c4. For the price of a pawn Black has evicted his opponent from the centre and unleashed the dark-squared bishop and the rook. These two pieces combine to rule out the natural ♘d5 in view of ...♖xb2. Moreover there is no time for 24 b3 in view of 24...e3! 25 ♕e1 e2 etc. Consequently Black's d-pawn is ready to run.

The game continued 24 a3 d5 25 g4 (with the prospect of being overrun in the middle of the board White hopes to undermine Black's pawns) 25...d4 26 ♖fe1 e3 27 ♕d3 fxg4 28 ♗e4 ♖xf4 29 ♖f1 ♖bf8 30 ♖xf4 ♖xf4 31 ♖f1 ♕f7 and Black was winning. Notice how quickly the tone (and direction) changed once Black had removed the central restraint. And herein lies the psychological factor – noticing is one thing, but fully appreciating the relevance of this example in terms of deepening one's relationship with an opening or defence is imperative on two interlinked fronts. Just as we should assume that our opponents are not going to hand us victory on a silver platter, as we progress it is also important to approach each game with the attitude that a certain amount of theoretical knowledge will play a part on both sides. The nature and extent of such a weapon is, of course, very significant, and in the most part players tend to allow the scope of their opening preparation to be limited by its definition, learning by heart a good number of variations which come to an abrupt end with an assessment. We are all guilty of this! Occasionally, with the fiery Sicilian Dragon, for example, even youngsters will venture as far as the 30th move (and more!) in their quest to fine-tune preparation, but this is usually a number-crunching exercise and has little to do with the actual character of the opening. We do learn tricks and ideas that hover in the background during the early phase because these are given or explained in specialist openings books or are found in notes and sub-notes in *ECO* etc. But the mass of characteristics of an opening exist way into the middlegame and the ending beyond.

Authors stress that we should play through 'random' games from international competition in order to get a feel for these variation-related themes that are an integral part of a particular line, but such sound advice is usually ignored and considered to be insufficiently relevant. This conscious decision to literally restrict work on openings to the actual opening moves is one of the most serious mistakes a player can make (which is why this subject is touched upon more than once in these pages). In fact concentrating on the quantity of variations 'learned' (remembered) rather than on the quality of an appreciation of the themes and concepts that will inevitably be experienced when we finally sit down to play could well be a psychological handicap. Of course it is a practical necessity to store theory, but doing so at the expense of understanding is sure to lead to the all too familiar situation of (after fifteen or twenty moves) arriving at an early middlegame with little or no idea as to what to do next!

Think of all the times we have heard (or come up with!) the excuse for losing the thread of the game so early as being due to the opponent unsportingly playing a move that is 'not theory' – or at least not known to us – but still quite playable, after which we have to think for ourselves. As the game progresses from the opening and deep into the middlegame we can't find a plan, don't know which pieces to exchange or keep, can't get our centre rolling despite the fact that we've seen a GM game in which he won easily doing just that... meanwhile our opponent seems to know which factors are relevant and has no problem steering the game in directions of his choosing. This can be a debilitating psychological blow – how come we can be dictated to by a player who doesn't even 'know' as much theory as we do? Our pre-game body armour has been ripped away. But we won't be so unlucky next time...

Yes we will. Until we take the time to

grow better acquainted with a particular line this will happen again and again, usually against opponents whose preparation involves studying games rather than remembering parts of games. We call our favourite openings and variations 'pet' lines, so we should try to understand them as we would a pet!

Anyway, let us now return to the initial position:

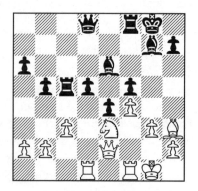

Black to move

If you were convinced by my positionally oriented case for White earlier, the example that followed should have served to alter such an assessment. Now we know that Black has an effective way to treat this situation in the – in hindsight – logical, thematic sacrifice of the b-pawn.

22...b4!

The game continued as follows:

23 cxb4 ♖c6 24 g4

Even White's reaction is the same! 24 ♘c2 d4.

24...fxg4 25 ♗xg4 d4! 26 ♗xe6+ ♖xe6 27 ♕c4 ♕c8 28 ♕xc8 ♖xc8 29 ♘f5 d3

Black suddenly has two connected passed pawns marching down the mid-

dle of the board.

30 ♖d2 ♗f8 31 a3 a5 32 bxa5 ♗c5+ 33 ♔g2 ♖f8 34 ♘g3 ♖d8 35 b4 e3

Now White tried **36 ♖xd3 ♖xd3 37 bxc5** but **37...♖c3 38 ♖e1 ♖xc5 39 ♔f3 ♖c3 40 ♖e2 ♖xa3 41 ♘f1 ♖xa5 42 ♘xe3 ♖a3 43 ♔f2 ♔f7** simplified to an ending that Black converted on the 69th move.

Now imagine, after learning a few lines of the Sveshnikov, sitting on Black's side of the board in a tournament or match game. The clock is ticking so there is not much time to devote to specific variations – particularly complex ones – and with which to formulate long-term plans and make subsequent assessments of future positions. A practical thought process would be similar to the one we started with, concentrating on White's apparent control of the centre and his structural advantage. Of course Black has active pieces and the lone dark-squared bishop, but generating piece play (or – less likely – using the centre pawns) might take some time. Trying to loosen White's grip by pushing the b-pawn comes to mind, but such a policy requires accurate analysis and might just lose material, so is easy to dismiss.

But the story would be much different if we had had the luxury of seeing what happened in the Tseshkovsky-Kharlov game when Black did sacrifice the b-pawn. Then such a possibility would already have formed part of our pre-game analysis, a key feature of the opening that falls within a range of scenarios and options whose scope is determined only by the extent to which we have prepared. The more we study relevant games the greater our range of options when we sit down to play. The overall psychological effect of such work can be immense. It is no coincidence that Kasparov is considered by many to be the best prepared player in the world, and I doubt he ends his theoretical preparation after fifteen moves!

Even if we know something about a particular line this does not mean we can go off in a new direction that might be the latest theoretical recommendation without a little extra homework. The following episode from the great Mikhail Tal's younger days should serve as a warning against insufficient preparation.

Before my game with Gipslis I was preparing for my University State Exam in Russian... so I was surrounded by some ten kilos of specialist literature. But suddenly the doorbell rang, and the postman arrived with, besides the rest of the mail, the latest issue of Shakhmatny Bulletin. I decided that fate itself was calling me to relax, so I lay down in a hot bath and began reading the magazine. Straight away I came across an article by N.Krogius on a topical variation of the Sicilian Defence. At that time I readily played this line both as White and Black, and here I suddenly read: 'Recently Black has frequently adopted the new continuation ...e5'. There followed two games, one of which Black won, while the second was drawn.

That's excellent, I thought, I'll have a quick draw in this variation with Gipslis, and then return to Philology.

As if it had been pre-arranged, inside five minutes we had played the moves of the variation given in the article, but when I made the 'recommended' move ...e5, a thought suddenly struck me: but what if White plays simply

♗*c4? Gipslis, however, did not give me time to torture myself mentally, but straight away made this move. The game continued for the full five hours, after which I had a hopeless position, and all that I achieved was an adjournment.*

The following morning I passed my exam, but resigned the game, whereupon we began analysing it. The first question that Gipslis asked was:

'Didn't you get the bulletin then?'

'Yes, why shouldn't I have?'

Here he took the bulletin out of his briefcase, showed me the move ...e5, then turned over a page (!), whereupon I read the very first line: 'However, by answering ...e5 with ♗c4, White sets his opponent difficult problems.'

Since then I have never prepared for a game while lying in a hot bath...

Style

What is your style of playing chess? Are you aggressive, positional, circumspect, cavalier, strategic, an endings expert, uncompromising, calm, nervous, theoretical...? Initially this seems like a simple question, for over the years or after a certain number of games we become accustomed to playing more in one particular fashion than others, results might seem related to specific opening systems (we might, for example, have excellent results against the French Defence) or other players might 'notice' that we defend well and rarely initiate tactics. However, whereas a football player, for instance, can quite accurately be described as a defender, attacking midfielder, striker and so on based on his allotted 'zone' of the playing field and the well defined role to which he tends to be assigned, chess is such a rich game that, during a tournament or a season of matches, it is not unusual to find ourselves in all manner of situations – even from the same openings or defences. Therefore the 'tags' of aggressive or strategist are rather simplistic, so it is more important to think about with which kinds of situation you feel most and least comfortable. This is not a quick and easy process and your conclusions might change quite drastically (and often) before you establish a coherent 'big picture' of your individual chess tastes.

Take a look at the following four diagrams that feature positions reached in a fairly random selection of openings.

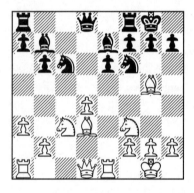

The diagram position is similar to a number of related situations with an isolated queen's pawn (IQP) that are experienced in several openings and defences. Chess players tend to fall into one of two categories – either we are more comfortable playing *with* an IQP or *against* one, and this preference is a good indication of a player's style.

In the diagram position aggressive players will see the d4-pawn as helping with White's space advantage, monitoring both c5 and e5 (which rules out the freeing ...e6-e5) and generally contribut-

ing to White's overall attacking stance. Of course we are aware of the fact that because it is isolated the d4-pawn is potentially vulnerable, and that the d5-square might (traditionally) prove useful to Black, but the former might not be relevant if White can generate kingside pressure, and White might be able to ignore Black's occupation of d5.

Karpov, on the other hand, would put his faith in structure and, given that Black is willing and able to withstand action against his king, wait patiently until the permanent nature of the IQP increases in significance. Ideally Black should be looking to relieve any tension through exchanges.

Chess is not that simple, of course, but even these general observations and preferences form the basis of a player's approach to the game and, subsequently, contribute to a fairly fundamental (perceived) categorisation regarding style and taste.

And what about the Botvinnik system of the Semi-Slav? If you're 'brave' enough to enter into this slugfest with either side, the chances are your first fifteen moves will go something like this: **1 d4 d5 2 c4 e6 3 ♘c3 ♘f6 4 ♘f3 c6 5 ♗g5 dxc4 6 e4 b5 7 e5 h6 8 ♗h4 g5 9 ♘xg5 hxg5 10 ♗xg5 ♘bd7 11 exf6 ♗b7 12 g3 c5 13 d5 ♕b6 14 ♗g2 0-0-0 15 0-0 b4**

Personally, I can safely say that this position does not suit my style whichever side of the board I could choose, and I guess that would be the case even for some players who categorise their style as aggressive and attacking. The tension here has already been cranked up to a high level.

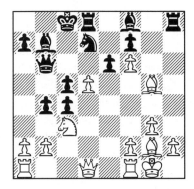

If one of the first moves that springs to mind is **16 ♖b1** because you have seen the variation **16...bxc3? 17 bxc3 ♕a6 18 ♖xb7 ♕xb7 19 dxe6** with a decisive advantage to White, then you might well like to try this opening out (with White or Black). Otherwise: be warned! In fact be warned anyway.

1 e4 e5, on the other hand, can set the game on the following path: **1 e4 e5 2 ♘f3 ♘c6 3 ♗c4 ♘f6 4 d3 ♗e7 5 0-0 0-0 6 ♗b3 d6 7 c3 ♘a5 8 ♗c2 c5 9 ♖e1 ♘c6 10 ♘bd2 ♖e8 11 ♘f1 h6 12 h3 ♗f8**

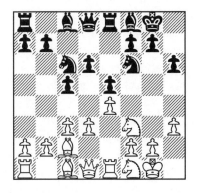

Clearly this kind of situation requires a patient approach where manoeuvring and gradual improvement of certain features are typical. The position is quite sober but, nonetheless, not without tension. A central pawn break with either d-pawn, for instance, can soon alter the flavour of the game, or if White is allowed to establish the dormant queen's knight on f5 and follow up with g2-g4 a dangerous kingside attack will be on the cards.

Positional, attacking (eventually) and generally flexible options are available to both sides, but this time the course of the game is in the hands of the players. The Botvinnik system scenario is quite different in that it is an example of the situation (to some extent) dictating the players, who did choose the opening initially but consequently find themselves at an irrevocable point where tactical motifs take over.

Or what about a juicy Sicilian Dragon if Black meets 1 e4 with 1...c5 and White opts for the 'open' 2 ♘f3 followed by 3 d4 cxd4 4 ♘xd4 and so on? **1 e4 c5 2 ♘f3 d6 3 d4 cxd4 4 ♘xd4 ♘f6 5 ♘c3 g6 6 ♗e3 ♗g7 7 f3 0-0 8 ♕d2 ♘c6 9 ♗c4 ♗d7 10 0-0-0 ♖c8 11 ♗b3 ♘e5 12 h4 h5 13 ♗g5 ♖c5 14 g4 hxg4 15 f4 ♘c4 16 ♕d3 b5**

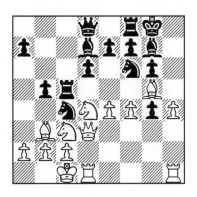

I can't vouch for the theory here – this is just a random selection from the sharp Yugoslav Attack beginning with 9 ♗c4. But is this your kind of game? Would you prefer to be sitting on White's side of the board, with your king under control and ready to break through on the h-file? Or are you spellbound by the Dragon bishop, primed for action on the long diagonal and working with the advanced knight, the queenside pawn(s) and the open c-file to attack White's king, which is clearly vulnerable!? Or – not unlikely – is this position simply too complex, too busy to allow for real chess?

And then there's all the theory to learn and the subtleties and nuances that inhabit each variation and sideline. If you want to take on the Sicilian you need to be ready for a host of other main lines from Black, while even if you think you could become an expert in the Dragon and can't wait for the next opponent to open 1 e4, what about 2 c3, 2 f4, 2 ♘f3 d6 3 ♗b5+/3 c3 or 3 d4 cxd4 4 ♕xd4 or other possibilities that are collectively very popular?

What these examples do demonstrate is that, whatever your style and taste, it is impossible to steer the game into channels that suit you every time you sit down to play. There are simply too many options available to both sides, regardless of how the game starts. And as sure as night follows day, every positional player favours an aggressive line somewhere in his repertoire, while tacticians will have a nice and tidy, quiet variation or pet defence tucked away. One of my teenage pupils (around 2000 Elo), for example, tends to shy away from adopting complex openings or systems when I first suggest them as a possible addition to his armoury, yet in recent years the Dragon and Benko have become the foundation of his repertoire with Black, and his latest 'pet' is 4 f3 against the Nimzo-Indian, an uncompromising line in which players such as Shirov – whose style is nothing like that of my young friend, who still believes his approach is far from aggressive – have led the way.

Remember that feeling comfortable in a certain kind of situation and being able to play it well don't necessarily go together, while appreciating why you don't like White's side of the IQP scenario, for example, does not mean you are unable to competently play appropriately. Flexibility is the key – strong players are so because their ability to adapt to a whole range of situations leaves them able to approach, for example, a middlegame with which they are not too well acquainted or comfortable with confidence, rather than with the familiar feeling of unease that accompanies our thoughts when the game has been hijacked and taken into hitherto uncharted territory.

Chess is like a box of chocolates – something for everyone, and you'll be surprised which ones you do and don't like.

It is interesting how even the very best players have styles so different that they would approach the same position with entirely contrasting styles. This is because chess is a game very rich in possibilities, with something to appeal to diverse tastes. Consequently Player A might focus on a weak square or enemy pawn with a view to a long-term positional bind, whereas Player B's attention might be drawn to tactical motifs around the enemy king. Player C could be more interested in the prospects of a minor piece ending in order to exploit the advantage of a long-range bishop over a knight, and will therefore look to trade pieces. Player D...

Fischer-Larsen
Candidates Semi-Final, Denver 1971

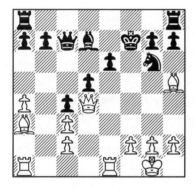

White to move

Put yourself in White's shoes here. What do you think of the position? White has the bishop pair, control of the dark squares, active pieces (centralised queen), a rock solid king position and a potential attack against Black's king. I would guess that most players would look at the pinned knight, Black's king, the backward e6-pawn and the pawns it supports and jump into action with Fischer's aggressive thrust.

18 f4

Typical Fischer, whose direct style favoured attacking options that put the opposition under pressure thanks to his ability to cut through complex varia-

tions in an almost clinical fashion. Already Black is faced with the prospect of what is left of his defences crumbling and having to defend in an open position. However, in his excellent *The Art of Chess Analysis* Timman proposes that Karpov or Romanishin would prefer 18 ♖e3 or perhaps 18 ♖e5, concentrating on the dark squares (maybe combined with the trade on g6) and not opening the position. I think that my style would be categorised as positional, but I must say that Fischer's choice appeals to me more than these two moves. Why is this? One reason, of course, is that this is someone else's game which I have the luxury of following in the pages of a book, and were I to find myself looking at the same position across the board in an actual game (and with Larsen sitting opposite me!), then I would probably settle for the less adventurous 18 ♖e3. It is difficult to say, but the very fact that 18 f4 seems perfectly natural to me when not under any pressure to perform is significant in itself. Anyway, let us look at how the players dealt with the rising tension.

18...♖he8 19 f5 exf5 20 ♕xd5+

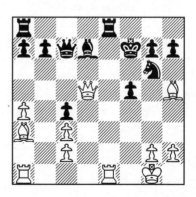

The first phase (at least since we

joined the game) is complete in that Black's king is quickly under fire.

20...♔f6

Not 20...♗e6 21 ♖xe6 ♖xe6 22 ♕xf5+ ♖f6 23 ♕d5+ ♖e6 24 ♖f1+ etc.

21 ♗f3! ♘e5! 22 ♕d4 ♔g6 23 ♖xe5 ♕xe5

23...♖xe5 24 ♗d6 etc.

24 ♕xd7 ♖ad8 25 ♕xb7 ♕e3+ 26 ♔f1 ♖d2

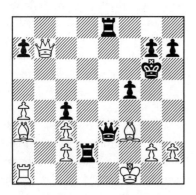

And this is the type of position you may well find yourself in if you have a no-nonsense attacking style! You can't make an omelette without breaking eggs, as they say. Perhaps it is a fear of – or lack of confidence in – dealing with these cut-throat situations that would lead me to chickening out of 18 f4 in a real game. Certainly Karpov prefers to keep the game within a more limited boundary of control and, although he is obviously capable of defending any such position, tends to find himself addressing dangerous-looking threats so far in advance (the text featured in Fischer's analysis before he embarked on this course) much less often than out and out aggressive players.

27 ♕c6+ ♖e6 28 ♗c5!

Great stuff! The problem for anyone who thinks that 18 f4 fits in best with their style is the subsequent necessity to find moves like ♗c5 here. On the other hand, the problem for anyone who opens 1 ♘f3, 2 g3, 3 ♗g2, 4 0-0 before even thinking about what to do with the centre pawns (by then the decision might be made for you) and with the intention of having a nice, positional, peaceful masterpiece, is that you rarely get to experience the excitement like the diagram above. Variety is the spice of life.

28...♖f2+ 29 ♔g1 ♖xg2+ 30 ♔xg2 ♕d2+ 31 ♔h1 ♖xc6 32 ♗xc6 ♕xc3?

32...a5! 33 ♗d4 ♔h6 34 ♖g1 g5 is preferable.

33 ♖g1+ ♔f6 34 ♗xa7 g5 35 ♗b6 ♕xc2 36 a5

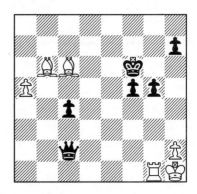

White will win the race.

36...♕b2 37 ♗d8+ ♔e6 38 a6 ♕a3 39 ♗b7 ♕c5 40 ♖b1 c3 41 ♗b6 1-0

Elsewhere in this book you will find a couple of examples and words of wisdom from Gligoric, whose pragmatic approach to chess deserves the greatest respect. About the opening phase of the game he wrote in his aptly titled *I Play Against Pieces*: 'My ethical obligation is to pay special attention to opening play. Chess laws are ruled by logic and only if the beginning of the game is irreproachable can other phases of the game create from it a beautiful, perfect whole.' Dedicating time and effort to opening play does not mean robotically remembering theory (I won't apologise for the number of times you might read such a line in these pages), rather thinking clearly and logically in readiness for the struggle ahead. Here is an example of how the man who was proclaimed the 'Yugoslav chess player of the 20th century' in a television poll produced a new idea in the complex King's Gambit.

Planinc-Gligoric
Ljubljana 1977

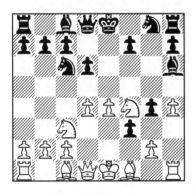

Black to move

9...f2+

Gligoric: "I realised that White had played very energetically to achieve a positional advantage and that special measures were needed for Black to gain counterplay, so, 'all by itself' an idea occurred to me and upon which I did

not hesitate for more than a couple of minutes... Hort said 'No!' when, after the game, out of curiosity I asked him if anything similar had ever occurred in the King's Gambit in the past." This comment is interesting indeed when taken in the context of his 'My ethical obligation...' contribution, above. One would assume that, at this level – particularly where the King's Gambit (as Black!) is concerned – top GMs would make sure they were intimately acquainted with whatever theory there is available before sitting down to play. But here we are, after only nine moves of one of the most complicated, uncompromising openings, witnessing an experienced and very strong GM approaching the situation as he would in the middlegame – actually thinking. Theoretical trends are of no concern to him. What matters is locking on to a logical mode of play with which he feels comfortable.

10 ♔xf2! g3+! 11 ♔xg3 ♞f6 12 ♗e2

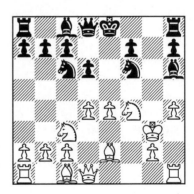

12...♖g8+

12...♞g4! 13 ♗xg4 ♖g8 14 ♔f2 ♗xg4 is more precise according to Gligoric.

13 ♔f2 ♘g4+ 14 ♗xg4 ♗xg4 15 ♕d3 ♗g7!

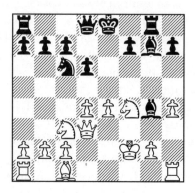

Forcing White to obstruct his own third rank and defending f6 in preparation for the next part of the plan.

16 ♗e3

16 d5 ♘e5.

16...♕d7

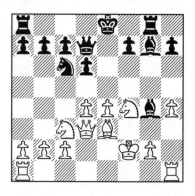

This is what Black had been aiming for with his double pawn sacrifice. White's king came under further pressure after Black castled queenside and opened another key file with ...f7-f5! In fact Black's play here was a product of a general, matter-of-fact observation he makes regarding a fundamental inconvenience White experiences in this opening: 'White's task of recovering the

gambit pawn can involve a particular weakening of the white kingside...' – rather obvious, perhaps, but it is how we interpret such pointers over the board that counts. Success is determined in no small part by the manner in which we translate our understanding of ostensibly simple observations (our own as well as those of others) into actual play, and there is just as much call for this in the opening as other parts of the game. Such independent thinking, moulding your play around your own style instead of copying others, is the only way of reaching positions that best suit your strengths and weaknesses. Of course your play must be sound but, over time, your understanding will improve along with your experience. I am not advocating taking on the King's Gambit or other fiery openings and defences with a bare minimum of theoretical homework and maximum reliance on natural ability and common sense. That would be risky even on a good day! But this example does serve to highlight the practical – and with it psychological – importance of including your style, taste, understanding and other aspects specific to your chess personality in the list of ingredients that blend to create a game of chess.

On a more realistic level, for example, is a pet line of one of England's thinking GMs, Keith Arkell. Well known for his endings expertise and deep positional understanding, Arkell is a perfect role model for those of you who see the modern 'requirement' for an encyclopaedic knowledge of opening theory as a factor quite removed from 'real' chess. Arkell's 'Speckled Egg' speciality is, ironically, a good try at making a chess omelette without breaking a single egg! It goes, quite simply, 1 d4 ♘f6 2 ♘f3 g6 3 b4!?

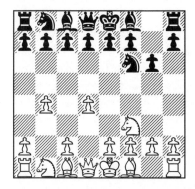

White stakes a claim for queenside space but not for an advantage. Instead Arkell has investigated the flavour, direction, structural, positional and other strategic aspects of the various directions the game can take from here and, confident that these suit his style and understanding well, is sufficiently armed for battle.

Again – please don't see this as a recommendation (although it does cut down on booking up on the King's Indian and Grünfeld if you play 1 d4), rather look for ways to build your opening repertoire to your own design as opposed to being too influenced by chess fashion.

Sense of Danger

Tigran Petrosian might not be one of the most well-known world champions among club players – certainly not the younger generation! – but he is considered to have had a particularly acute sense of danger. Most of us have experienced a feeling of satisfaction, of being wiser than our contemporaries, after deciding against a promising looking, desirable line because it didn't quite 'feel' right at the crucial time, only to learn after the game that we were indeed correct to be cautious. However, most of us have also experienced that feeling of terrible disappointment, embarrassment... even shame(!) after deciding to go ahead with a promising looking, desirable line despite the fact that it didn't quite 'feel' right at the crucial time, only to learn after just a few moves that, once again, we failed to err on the side of caution. Unfortunately the latter case has far more relevance to our chess career than the former! These dispiriting reverses tend to result from our endeavours to carry out a would-be thematic plan or an integral part of a standard strategy – even after a potential danger has been checked out. Not surprisingly we are most at risk of falling foul of our insisting on a particular course of action – the execution of which is often a focal point around which a game revolves – when among its consequences are newly opened lines and tactical possibilities. Here is such a natural example.

Tischbierek-Hertneck
German Championship 2001

A brief appraisal of the diagram position draws our attention to two key features – Black's rather vulnerable-looking kingside and the backward e6-pawn. Although not particularly serious, these factors do appear to outweigh the isolated d4-pawn, which anyway serves a purpose by monitoring e5, the traditionally important square in such a scenario.

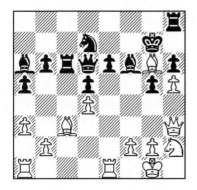

Black to move

A closer look sees that White's queen hits the e6-pawn along with the rook on e1, which also adds to White's control of e5, as does the bishop that has just arrived on c3. Meanwhile White's knight is just one step away from exerting further pressure on e5. Notice that in terms of attack and defence Black has the e6-pawn sufficiently covered, so something like 28...♖hc8 followed, perhaps, by ...♘f8 is a solid enough way to continue, giving e6 extra protection, evicting the bishop from g6 and reminding White who has the most presence on the queenside. Yet again it is easy to be level-headed after the event, but in practice we tend not to be too happy nursing long-term weaknesses such as a backward e6-pawn, rather we are constantly on the lookout for ways in which to rid ourselves of the burden with ...e6-e5 which, not untypically, could well lead to an advantage. Not surprisingly, then, Black, who has no doubt been aware of the implications of his potential liability – and the significance of its advance – thus far,

cance of its advance – thus far, was trying to make the ...e6-e5 advance work here. Why stay 'passive' with ...♖fc8, for example, when there is an option to break out in the centre, unleashing our pieces in the process? Moreover, the only obstacle seems to be White's dark-squared bishop, which looks quite defensive on c3 but might have something dangerous in store in the event of the opening of the long diagonal – on which stands Black's king – after ...e6-e5 and d4xe5. Therefore Black will have checked for tricks here and been relieved to find that nothing works for White. Hence the game continued as follows:

28...e5?? 29 dxe5 ♘xe5

However, after the simple continuation **30 ♗xe5!** (not 30 ♖xe5? on account of 30...♖xc3!) **30...♗xe5 31 ♖xe5!** Black saw the error of his ways!

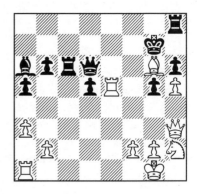

In fact Black resigned in view of 31...♕xe5 32 ♕d7+, when mate on f7 is inevitable. It is fitting that, to add insult to injury, apart from the final tactic of the game the flurry of action since Black confidently pushed his e-pawn all took place on the wholly appropriate e5-square! Presumably Black did focus on e5 as well as the a1–h8 diagonal, but he forgot about White's queen lurking on the edge of the board – a dangerous neglection indeed. Crucially, Black's 'freeing' plan also broke a rule – adhered to by pupils of the old Soviet Chess School – that advises us against opening the position when our king is susceptible to attack. This possibility in itself should have set the alarm bells ringing, particularly in view of the fact that White's bishop is the closest piece to Black's king. Moreover, White's king, in contrast, is perfectly safe, so even more vigilance is required from Black. I suppose we should factor into the equation the possibility of time-trouble, although this, too, should serve to heighten our sense of danger rather than relax it. Returning to the initial diagram, Black might have wanted to break out with the e-pawn rather than be tied to its defence, but this desire seems to have taken priority over practical considerations, namely safety.

I Made Too Many Wrong Mistakes...
When there is a decent-looking alternative to a committal move it is prudent to keep your powder dry. Of course this sounds obvious as we read these words now – the problem is practising what we preach when sitting at the board, with the clock running, adrenalin flowing and emotions taking their toll! Both my own experience and conversations with other players suggest that it pays to try to be aware of our dubious chess tendencies and weaknesses so that when these potentially hazardous possibilities present themselves we are ready to properly weigh up the pros and cons.

My advice throughout this book is generally to make an effort to know yourself in order to be well armed psychologically, as is the case here. By merely making a mental note of the words 'sense of danger' earlier in this chapter we are already putting in place in our subconscious a 'danger tag' that will be activated each time a relevant situation arises. Incidentally, looking at what happened from White's point of view, it is worth remembering Black's psychology here. When your opponent is looking to break out of what seems a cramped position, keep an eye on the possibilities, especially if captures are involved. And since chess is essentially a battle of wills in which one player tries to frustrate the plans of another, the fact that you have been trying to prevent a pawn break, for example, often makes an opponent even more intent on making it work, and consequently more inclined to ignore the danger signals. Perhaps this was another factor in our current example, as Black pushed his e-pawn immediately White had posted another piece within range of e5.

When contemplating a radical alteration of circumstances brought about by a forcing sequence of captures, the fact that we are instigating this change in direction can lead us to believe that our 'authority' continues after the forced variation has ended. This is a common and hazardous example of overconfidence that can lead to trouble, and the best way to avoid such a mishap is to pay special attention to the position that arises as soon your opponent is no longer required to dance to your tune. Clearly we should be careful to check through any kind of sequence of captures, but a critical point of this kind of analysis is at the end! After the target move, when the mission has been accomplished, that is when something unpleasant might come back at us, either in the form of an unwelcome surprise resource or – equally serious – a completely inaccurate (over-ambitious) assessment of the resulting position. Watch White spoil his own party here.

Platonov-Zaitsev
USSR Championship, Riga 1970

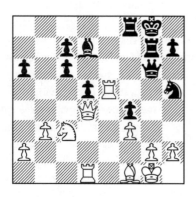

White to play

White is a pawn down but it appears to have been a sacrifice since his positional compensation is worth more. Basically, Black has four pawn islands to White's more attractive two, with the resulting long-term weaknesses on a6, c6 (c7) and f4. Meanwhile the consequential c5-square looks particularly inviting for White's knight, and White also enjoys the more active pieces. In fact with his kingside quite safe White can claim an advantage. However, White allowed himself to be tempted by the apparently hanging knight on h5

and thus embarked on the following forcing line.

25 ♘xd5? cxd5 26 ♕xd5+ ♔h8 27 ♖xh5

White has succeeded, as planned, in converting the comfortable positional plus into a material lead whilst maintaining the superior structure. Unfortunately he failed to properly consider the situation after the capture on h5...

27...♗c6! 28 ♕e5 ♗xf3

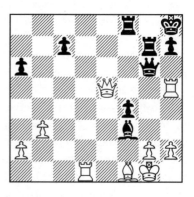

Oh dear! Never be too satisfied with your mini-achievements during a game. When you come to the end of a forcing variation that you initiated, start afresh from there with a different, more cautious perspective. It is a distinctly unsatisfying feeling to see the game disintegrate in front of your eyes when your opponent has managed only to find a single move of his own after been taken along for the ride. Beware deceptively inviting, favourable simplifying lines!

Our sense of danger can be particularly distant when matters appear to be well under our control and very few pieces remain on the board. Let us put ourselves in Black's shoes in the following position:

Czebe-Koneru
Budapest 2001

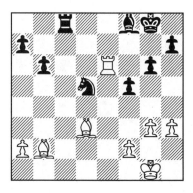

Black to move

Black has an extra pawn for which White's albeit insufficient compensation is the bishop pair. With this in mind Black could have considered 28...♔f7 29 ♖e2 ♗g7!, when 30 ♗xg7 ♔xg7 simply allows Black to safely maintain her material advantage, e.g. 31 ♖e5 ♖c5 etc.

Instead there followed:

28...♘b4 29 ♗b5 ♖c2?! 30 ♖e2

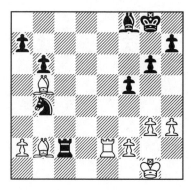

Again Black would have stood clearly better after 30...♗g7!? to trade bishops or assume control of the diagonal. Would you have contested the long di-

agonal? Or would you have simplified with the more natural trade of rooks? Koneru opted for the latter...

30...♖xe2?? 31 ♗c4+! 1-0

I am sometimes guilty of advising my very young pupils that by exchanging queens they immediately rule out two possible disasters – blundering their queen(!) and allowing a silly mate by the enemy queen. In reality, of course, disasters can happen at any time, and instead of the automatic recapture the crafty Mr Czebe decided to throw in a bombshell of a check... Unfortunately for Black the prospect of grinding out a win after eventually making the extra pawn tell suddenly went up in smoke to be replaced by the very immediate prospect of being mated in an ending in which the victor has only two pieces still in play! Perhaps you think 'unfortunately for Black' is too kind for one of the strongest women in history, who should know better than to allow what appears to be a simple mate. Perhaps, but it is what caused this terrible blunder that is of interest to us. One possibility is the fact that Black had been aware all along of the danger posed by the raking bishops, didn't worry about the check on c4 because the square was defended by the rook and then forgot about it altogether when trading on e2. Or maybe she thought that the rook was still on c2 (a common mirage), or even – thanks to 'automatic' mode – imagined that ♖xe2 was 'forced' and there was time to address the check on the next move. Easily done! Alternatively the mate element of the check might not have entered her thoughts because the focus of her attention was the a2-pawn. In itself the aggressive 29...♖c2 suggests that Black had the enemy queenside in her sights, so it is not unlikely that this prompted her to channel her analysis and see that 31 ♖xe2 ♘xa2?? is not on because the knight drops after the fork on c4 – highlighting the 'wrong' feature of the bishop's arrival on c4. Again this is easily done, and it even includes a measure of logic that can be enough to cause such blindness. But that is still no excuse, I hear you cry. And I agree, but who has never fallen for a bolt-from-the-blue and completely avoidable mate?! As usual we need to remind ourselves of our fallibility, and nobody – Kasparov included – is above a little mental reminder that might mean mechanically monitoring, for example, obvious checks. I also urge my little pupils to carry out a simple safety procedure before making a move in order to avoid something very nasty happening. Yet again this seems such an obvious thing to do, but we tend to be guilty of not bothering with methodical processes once we reach a certain playing level. For Kasparov, of course, these mental checks are second nature!

Natural but not Best

Analyse the following position for 20-30 seconds...

Black has just played 13...exd4. How would you recapture here? The vast majority of club players would almost automatically play 14 ♘xd4 as the alternative voluntarily surrenders what appears to be a decent dark-squared bishop.

Gligoric-V.Kovacevic
Pula 1981

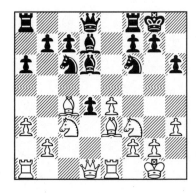

White to move

Given the context of this printed page and the question itself, I suppose there will be more takers for the correct **14 ♗xd4!**, which wins control of the e5-square and therefore allows White to stamp his authority in the centre. The game continued **14...♘xd4 15 ♕xd4** (the point, and not altogether obvious) **15...b5 16 ♗a2 ♘h7 17 e5 ♗e7 18 ♖ad1 ♗c6 19 ♕e3 ♕e8 20 e6 f5**

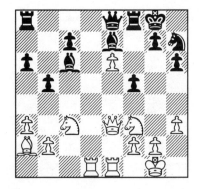

Thanks to White's vision of the 'bigger picture' he now has an enormous, protected passed pawn in the heart of enemy territory. Such a significant advantage won't come your way in these circumstances if you adhere too closely to the stereotyped thinking regarding the general superiority of bishops over knights. Anyway, it is worth looking at the finish: **21 ♘d5 f4 22 ♕c3** (threatening 23 ♕xc6 ♕xc6 24 ♘xe7+) **22...♗xd5 23 ♗xd5 ♖d8 24 ♗c6 ♕h5 25 ♖d7 ♖xd7 26 exd7 ♗d8 27 ♖e8 ♘f6 28 ♕b3+ ♕f7 29 ♕xf7+ ♔xf7 30 ♘e5+ 1-0**

Here's a funny one from a strong 2500 player.

Braun-Rabiega
German Championship 2001

Black to move

White threatens to severely disrupt Black's king by lifting the g7-pawn after forcing the bishop from g6 with f4-f5. Atlas recommends 39...f6 40 ♘f3 ♖e7 with 'good counterchances' but we can understand why Rabiega chose not to play this because, apart from the slight weakening of the pawn structure, Black's queen is tied down to the defence of the bishop. Why be subject to such inconvenience when the g-pawn can be protected simply and without

compromising the kingside with...
39...♖g8??

The answer, alas, comes with White's reply...
40 f5! 1-0

Black resigned as 40...♗xf5 walks into immediate mate on h5. Well, it is not as if Black was not ready for the threatened (telegraphed!) push of the f-pawn! Nor will he have missed the fact that the h-pawn is hanging after ...♗xf5, but when we joined the game Black would have dropped his king back to g8 with a decent game. Consequently, since parting with the h-pawn is not a problem for Black, he will have concentrated almost exclusively on the fate of the g-pawn, comparing the line beginning 39...f6 with the text. Of course this would have been fine were it not for the rook leaving the king dangerously short of breathing space. And this is the factor that should have alerted Black to why the awkward-looking ...♖g8 is awkward-looking – because we rarely follow kingside castling with choosing g8 as an outpost for the rook! Doing so, surely, can lead only to trouble... Just as 'good moves play themselves' and 'sound positions create good moves' and so on, it is worth remembering that 'odd moves can lead to trouble' – particularly if your kingside is under scrutiny. It is interesting to note from these examples that blunders have come from very respectable players after ostensibly clear and reasoned thought! In other words, it can happen to all of us, so we should not be fooled into believing life is good just because we navigate our way through a couple of variations. Be alert – be very alert!

Think like Fritz!

Wouldn't it be nice if we had a super-human ability to – despite the often rising tension in a game – detach ourselves from all the complications and zone straight in on the strongest, most logical move...

J.Horvath-Antal
Budapest 2001

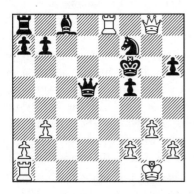

White to move

Thanks to the pin on the 8th rank White should be on his way to victory. Thus the game continued as follows:

27 ♖xc8?

This is obvious and maintains White's winning chances, but there is a more accurate move that has the enormous advantage of minimising Black's counterplay and, consequently, making the winning task simpler. First let's see what happened in the game.

27...♖xc8 28 ♕xc8 ♘g5

There is nothing else, but the light squares are inviting in any case. The text is more of an inconvenience to White than a genuine threat to his netting the full point. Nonetheless, who wants inconvenience?

29 ♕c3+ ♔g6

30 h4?!

Another move which does not throw away the win but further complicates the process. Black's knight will dance around anyway, so better is 30 ♖c1. Then 30...♘f3+ (30...♘h3+ 31 ♔f1 ♕h1+ 32 ♔e2 ♘g1+ 33 ♔d2 ♕d5+ 34 ♕d3 ♘f3+ 35 ♔e3) 31 ♔g2 ♘d2+ (31...♘h4+ 32 ♔f1 ♘f3 33 ♕e3 ♘xh2+ 34 ♔e2; or 31...♘e1+ 32 ♔f1 ♘d3 33 ♖d1 ♕h1+ 34 ♔e2 ♕e4+ 35 ♔d2 ♘xf2 36 ♖e1) 32 f3! (32 ♔h3 ♘e4) 32...♘xf3! 33 ♕xf3 (33 ♕e3!?) 33...♕d2+ 34 ♔h3 ♕xc1 35 ♕xb7 ♕f1+ 36 ♕g2 leaves White a healthy pawn up, albeit in a notoriously complex queen and pawn ending (think of all those checks).

30...♘f3+ 31 ♔g2?

White has simply failed to cope with the constant pressure against his king, successive inaccuracies (the latest being the most serious) culminating in Black earning the draw through checks and threats. This time 31 ♔f1 ♘d4 32 f3 ♘xf3 33 ♖c1 ♘d2+ 34 ♔g1 ♘e4 (34...♘f3+ 35 ♔f2 ♘d2 36 ♕e3 ♘e4+ 37 ♔g1 transposes) 35 ♕e3 ♕e5 36 ♖c2! is the way to go, with a clear advantage.

31...♘xh4+ 32 ♔f1 ♘f3 33 ♔g2

33 ♕e3!? at least puts the onus on Black to find 33...♘d4 34 ♕e8+ ♔g5!, preventing ♕h5 (which would protect h1).

33...♘e1+!? 34 ♔f1 ♘c2!

It will be a pity to see the knight go, but the job is done.

35 ♕xc2 ♕h1+ 36 ♔e2 ♕xa1

Now Black had done enough to secure the draw.

Let us return to the initial position:

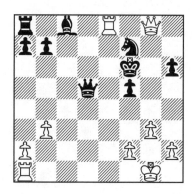

White to move

In hindsight we now know that, after picking up the bishop, White's life was made more difficult by the weaknesses in front of his king. I am sure that

White, if only briefly, looked for a possibility of addressing his kingside before playing ♖xc8, but this seems futile. Moreover, a few checks shouldn't take long to wriggle out of. However, the pin means that the bishop isn't going anywhere, so this should give us time to consider whether anything can be done to facilitate the winning process. In fact the solution is – surprise, surprise! – logical and quite simple yet far from obvious to find. Our attention is drawn to the f3-square...

27 ♖f1!!

This is more of a Fritz move, I admit, but it is straight to the point in that the pressure is maintained – note that the knight is also pinned – while White takes time to prepare a defence. Having played through the game continuation, can you see what the decisive difference would now be if it were White to play? First let us check out Black's defensive tries. 27...♕c6 (27...♕d7 28 ♖c1) 28 ♖f8 ♕c7 (28...♕e6 29 ♖c1) 29 ♕h8+ ♔e6 (29...♔g6 30 ♖g8+ ♔h5 31 ♕f6 leads to mate, and 29...♔e7 30 ♖xf7+ ♔xf7 31 ♕h7+ is final) 30 ♖e1+ and the end is approaching. So Black is in a helpless situation after 27 ♖f1!!, which brings us to the point behind the move: the threat is to follow 28 ♖xc8 ♖xc8 29 ♕xc8 ♘g5 30 ♕c3+ ♔g6 (as in the game) with 31 f3, immediately nipping in the bud any hope of counterplay from Black. This seems rather simple now, but the strong Hungarian GM failed to think so clearly during the game. Had he given more respect to his opponent's queen + knight team, then perhaps Horvath would have found ♖f1.

Chess is not an easy game, but singling out key squares, threats and relevant pieces and investigating how the implications of certain themes might be addressed can be broken down to what is actually a relatively simple process – at any level. As usual (and this advice deserves repeating), don't let the fact that you control the game allow you to be rushed into tidying up into the next phase. Any hint of counterplay should at least prompt you to search for preventative measures and, as this example illustrates, this can be surprisingly easy with a little clear thinking.

Schaller-M.Müller
Bundesliga 2001

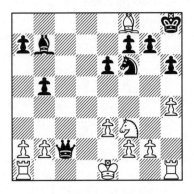

Black to move

White has two rooks for the queen but failure to castle means that these pieces have still not been introduced. In fact with White's king stuck in the centre Black seems to be in the driving seat. In what way would you be looking to exploit your current activity here?

Well, we are drawn to both b2, which is there for the taking, and f2, which certainly looks vulnerable. 22...♕xb2 23

0-0 ♗xf3 24 gxf3 nets a pawn and weakens White's kingside and should leave Black with an advantage, but White does have more pieces. Also favouring Black is 22...♘e4 23 0-0 ♕xb2. Less obvious is the attacking retreat with 22...♕g6 to hit g2 and concentrate on White's weaker colour complex. Then 23 ♘d4 ♕xg2 24 ♖f1 gives Black a pleasant choice, e.g. 24...♕h2 or 24...♘g4.

But Black was sufficiently open-minded to consider options other than the immediate tries, allowing his thoughts to feature his 'fourth' piece which, ironically, was able to make a near decisive contribution.

22...♔g8! 23 ♗e7

Suddenly the two forgotten pieces become the key players, for the attacked bishop finds itself without a safe square. 23 ♗d6 (trying to keep the bishop out of harm's way) 23...♘e4 and 23 ♗a3 ♗xf3 24 gxf3 b4! 25 ♗xb4 ♕xb2 invite Black to combine threats.

23...♘g4 24 ♘d2

Unfortunately for White the natural 24 0-0 runs into 24...♕c7!.

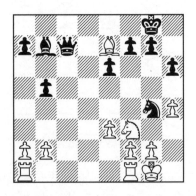

The point is that Black threatens ...♗xf3 followed by ...♕h2 mate while simultaneously hitting the hapless bishop. Black will have seen this possibility when he discovered ...♚g8, which is quite impressive because, even those of us who did consider nudging the king across and subsequently found how to deal with 23 ♗a3 and 23 ♗d6 probably came to the end of the line at 23 ♗e7. Even worse is 24 ♖f1 ♗xf3 25 gxf3 ♘e5 etc.

24...♛c7 25 ♗a3 ♗xg2 26 ♖g1 ♛h2 27 ♚e2 f5!

Reminding White of his unenviable predicament. The presence of opposite-coloured bishops renders White's defensive task almost impossible because he cannot contest the light squares. The text leaves Black ready to hit f2 by dropping back the bishop or simply removing the h4-pawn in the event of 28 ♖ge1. Consequently White tries to put his troubled bishop to good use.

28 ♗d6 ♗f3+!

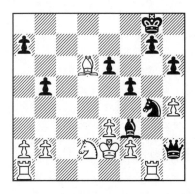

Thanks to Black's previous move 29 ♚xf3 walks into mate on f2.

29 ♘xf3 ♛xf2+ 30 ♚d3 ♛xe3+ 31 ♚c2 ♛xf3 32 ♗c5 ♛e2+ 33 ♚b3 ♛c4+ 34 ♚a3 ♛a4 mate

While there is no disputing Black's lead in the initial diagram it is worth noting the way in which Müller managed to zone in on the most direct route to victory, beginning with the star king move, featuring the theme involving ...♛c7 and including ...♗f3+ in the proceedings. We know that the king comes into its own in the ending but this 'rule' does not preclude considering this often forgotten piece in our calculations during other stages of the game, even – as in this case – when, in an attacking position, our attention is directed to the front pieces. No piece should be overlooked at any time!

Non-standard Opening Play

Almost all of us – myself included – have only a limited amount of time away from work, school or life in general in which to study openings. And, as I have said elsewhere in this book, appreciating the various positional, strategic, tactical and other kinds of aspects relevant to the opening or defence is just as important as the mechanical process of recalling recommended sequences and the evaluations that accompany them. Moreover, once the basic lines have been learned the 'real' chess makes all the difference. Since so many players don't use their time properly it pays to include in one's armoury a line or two designed to almost secretly throw the opponent off balance, to take the game down a non-standard but not unorthodox channel when it seems that a conventional course will be followed. In the following game Black adopts his King's Indian set-up against what is considered by most players to be a fairly insipid system, the Double Fianchetto, only to see White castle queenside.

Badea-Jianu

Rumanian Championship 2001

Double Fianchetto

1 ♘f3 ♘f6 2 g3 g6 3 b3 ♗g7 4 ♗b2 0-0 5 ♗g2 d6 6 d4 e5 7 dxe5 ♘fd7

A standard means of contesting the centre with which Black tends to expect to earn approximate equality.

8 ♘c3 dxe5 9 ♕d2

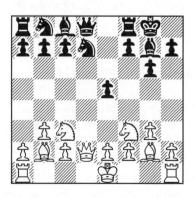

But White prepares to castle long!

9...♘c6

White will also send his king west in reply to alternatives: 9...♘a6 10 0-0-0 ♕e7 11 h4 h6 (11...h5!?) 12 h5 g5 13 ♘d5 ♕d6 14 ♘xg5!

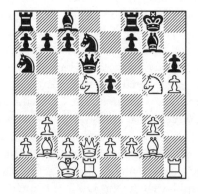

This is a good example of how diffi-

cult the game can be for Black, e.g. 14...hxg5 15 h6 (15 ♕xg5 ♕h6) 15...♗f6 16 h7+ ♔g7 17 f4! with a dangerous attack, or 14...c6 15 ♕d3 hxg5 16 h6 as in Sulava-Mazi, Velden 1996, which continued 16...♗f6 17 ♘xf6+ ♕xf6 18 h7+ ♔h8 19 ♕e3 ♕g7 20 f4 f6 21 fxg5 fxg5 22 ♖xd7 ♗xd7 23 ♕xe5! 1-0

Another line is 9...♖e8 10 0-0-0. Then 10...e4 11 ♘e1 ♕f6 12 ♕e3 ♘b6 13 ♘d3! ♕e7 14 ♘f4 was clearly better for White in Sulava-Armanda, Pula 1999, as was 11 ♘d4 e3 12 fxe3 c6 13 e4 ♘a6 14 g4 ♕h4 15 h3 ♘ac5 16 ♔b1 ♘f6 17 ♕f4 ♘e6 18 ♘xe6 ♗xe6 19 ♖hf1 in L.Hansen-Joecks, Germany 1997. Perhaps best is 10...a5, when Dizdar-Fercec, Nova Gorica 1997 went 11 h4 a4 12 h5 axb3 13 axb3 e4 14 ♘g5 e3 15 ♕d5 ♕f6 16 hxg6 hxg6 17 f4 c6 18 ♕d3 ♘f8 19 ♘ge4 ♖xe4 20 ♗xe4 ♖a2 21 ♕d8 with an unclear position.

10 0-0-0 a5 11 h4 a4?!

11...h5 holds back the h-pawn but weakens g5. Co.Ionescu-Gallagher, Istanbul Olympiad 2000, went 12 ♘g5 ♖a6 13 ♔b1 ♘d4 14 e3 ♘e6 15 ♘xe6 ♖xe6 16 ♘b5 a4 17 ♗h3 f5 18 e4 axb3 19 axb3 ♖b6 20 ♕e2 with an edge for

White. 11...h6 looks best, e.g. 12 g4 (12 h5 g5) 12...a4 13 g5 h5 14 e3 axb3 15 axb3 ♘b4 16 ♗h3 e4 17 ♗xd7 exf3 18 ♗xc8 ♕xc8 19 ♘d5 with a balanced game in Dizdar-Spasov, Yerevan 1996.

The common denominator here, of course, is the fact that the kings reside on opposite flanks, bringing about a situation not usually in keeping with a double fianchetto. Instead of the centre and the queenside coming under a little mild pressure, the kings are the focus of attention. This is the same for both players, but the psychological momentum is with White, whose favoured opening variation this is, and who, therefore, has the double luxury of experience and preparation. Black, meanwhile, will still be trying to adapt to White's king being on the 'wrong' flank.

12 h5

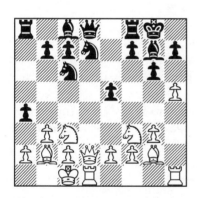

12 ♘xa4!? ♕e7 13 h5 ♖xa4 14 bxa4 ♘b6 15 hxg6 fxg6 (15...hxg6 16 ♕g5) 16 ♕c3 seems to leave Black with insufficient compensation.

12...axb3 13 axb3 ♕e7?!

Simplifying with 13...♘b6 14 ♕xd8 (14 ♕e3 ♕e7) 14...♖xd8 15 ♖xd8+ ♘xd8 is only slightly worse for Black.

The text leaves the queen rather exposed.

14 hxg6 hxg6

14...fxg6 runs into 15 ♖xh7! ♔xh7 16 ♘g5+ ♔g8 (16...♔h8 17 ♖h1+) 17 ♗d5+ etc.

15 ♘d5 ♕d6?!

As per plan – for both players. 15...♕d8 16 ♕c3 is a lesser evil.

16 ♕g5!

White simultaneously prepares an attack on the enemy queen while sending his own queen over to the kingside, just one step away from the open h-file. This is not an uncommon theme with this line and so in some way will have been part of White's analysis.

16...♖e8

16...♖a5 meets with 17 ♕h4 ♖e8 18 ♘b6 etc.

17 ♘b6! ♕xd1+ 18 ♖xd1 ♘xb6

White is too actively placed for Black to hope for compensation, and White won in another six moves. Obviously there are pros and cons to every system, so I am not recommending that everyone plays it, but this example does demonstrate the efficacy of giving a slightly different flavour to a conventional opening. A psychological edge

combined with rather promising opportunities on the board can be an enormous advantage.

Inducing Errors in Simple Positions

How many times against stronger opposition have you found yourself on the
wrong side of a difficult position without apparently being able to pinpoint a
genuine mistake? Too many. Games are
won and lost for a number of reasons,
but the ones that seem to rather annoy-
ingly drift away tend to do so as a result
of a long-term positional error – usually
one that is not forced.

Z. Varga-Bakre
Budapest 2001

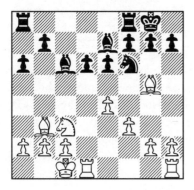

White to move

Here we have a typical Sicilian pawn
layout, with no serious weaknesses for
either side. The absence of queens does
make a difference but many other
pieces remain on the board so it is important to avoid making unnecessary
concessions. Our attention is drawn,
perhaps, to the d6-pawn because it is
protected by the bishop which also
supports the knight. Thus 15 ♗xf6

springs to mind, forcing Black to make
a decision. In fact after 15...♗xf6!? 16
♖xd6 ♗e5 Black's pawn investment
furnishes attractive compensation in the
form of a good deal of influence on the
dark squares now that White's bishop
has disappeared. This is a well-known
theme in the Sicilian (particularly with
this d6-e6 'small' centre) and Varga understandably turns down this possibility.
Nevertheless, this does not mean that
the d6-pawn is not worth putting under
a bit more pressure as it is a fairly easy
target.

15 ♖d3 ♖fe8!?

Given White's previous move this is
already a questionable choice as the d-
file seems to be a more appropriate location for the rook (the queen's rook
has a ready-made home on the c-file),
which might as well have gone to d8
immediately.

16 ♗f4!

I think White deserves praise for this
move for psychological reasons. There
is nothing special about the move in
itself but Black's latest hinted at what
now follows, which – I am sure – contributed to White's deciding on the text.
The d6-pawn is attacked and Black has
two choices: gain a tempo with ...e6-e5
and hope that the resulting hole on d5
won't be a problem or acknowledge
that ...♖fe8 was not the most accurate
with ...♖ed8, freeing e8 for the knight.
As admitting mistakes – particularly
when this means 'wasting a move' – can
be difficult, White exploits the fact that
the game is still in its opening phase,
with nothing yet happening, to essay a
sort of 50–50 chance...

16...e5?!

And is deservedly rewarded! White was alert to the signal and will now be able to focus on the d5-square for a while. This might not appear to be a serious weakness for Black, who seems to have been more concerned about being tied down to the defence of the d6-pawn, but short-term solutions that incur long-term positional/structural concessions should be avoided if possible, and Black is guilty of not appreciating the bigger picture here. Better is 16...♖ed8 17 ♖hd1 ♘e8 which looks passive but is quite solid.

Let us see how White now punished his opponent for volunteering the d5-square as an outpost.

17 ♗e3 ♗d7

The bishop heads for e6.

18 g4

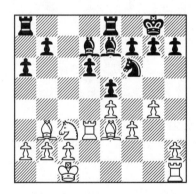

White also commits himself, but this thrust is aimed at dislodging the knight in order to accentuate White's grip on d5.

18...♗e6

18...h6 19 h4 helps only White.

19 g5

19 ♘d5 ♘xd5 20 ♗xd5 ♗xd5 21 ♖xd5 ♖ec8 favours White but the text is stronger.

19...♘d7

Suddenly Black is seriously outnumbered in terms of the increasingly relevant d5-square.

20 ♘d5 ♗d8 21 h4 ♘c5 22 ♗xc5

22 ♖d2 secures a comfortable advantage but this capture opens the d-file – which Black is ill-prepared to contest – and eliminates a decent piece while maintaining control of d5.

22...dxc5 23 ♘e3 ♗xb3 24 axb3

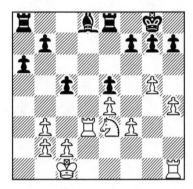

The simplification has left White with a clear advantage thanks to the d-file, the light squares, the superior minor piece and, of course, the d5-square. And all this because Black allowed his judgement to be clouded by a refusal to be flexible and by the false and immediate convenience of addressing the attack on his d-pawn with a tempo-gaining but committal advance in the centre. Remember – every pawn move creates a weakness.

As for White, he was alert to the possibility after noticing the potential implications of ...♖fe8, with which Black appeared to be signalling his intentions regarding the fate of his centre.

However, the story does not end here...

Can't See the Wood for the Trees

When a hitherto sweet-smelling game suddenly turns sour we tend to dwell on where we might have gone wrong, or we simply look down on the area of the board where the opponent has just turned the tables and see only these enemy pieces that have done – or are about to do – the damage. This is exactly what happened to Varga:

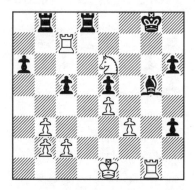

Black to move

We rejoin the Varga-Bakre game with White appearing to be in the driving seat thanks to his active rook on the seventh rank working well with the knight. However, Black used his cheeky passed pawn to execute an infiltration of his own.

33...h2 34 ♖h1 ♖d2

The point is that after 35 ♘xg5 ♖xc2! Black threatens the skewer on c1 as well as ...hxg5, e.g. 36 ♔d1 ♖xb2 37 ♔c1 ♖2xb3 etc.

Now the game continued **35 ♖g7+ ♔h8 36 ♘xg5 ♖xc2 37 ♖h7+ ♔g8 38 ♖xh6 ♖c1+ 39 ♔f2 ♖xh1 40 ♖g6+ ♔f8 41 ♔g2 ♖c1! 42 ♔xh2 ♖xb3 43 ♖xa6** (43 ♖f6+ ♔e7 44 ♖e6+ ♔d7 45 ♖xe5 ♖xb2+ 46 ♔g3 c4)

43...♖xb2+ 44 ♔h3 c4 45 ♔g4 c3 46 ♔f5 ♖cb1 47 ♔f6 ♖b6+ 48 ♘e6+ ♖xe6+ 0-1

Fair enough, but let's return to the position after 35...♔h8.

Of course it was appropriate that White's analysis revolved around ♘xg5 given that he is in trouble on the back rank whatever happens but, until ...♖d2 was played, it was White who was dreaming of glory on the seventh rank. We have seen that after ♘xg5 Black takes time to nudge his rook across to c2, so what about 36 ♖h7+ as a path to a bit of glory?

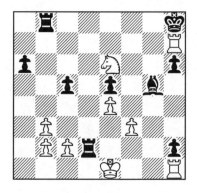

After 36...♔xh7 37 ♘xg5+ Black is too busy getting out of the check to save his rook, and the continuation 37...♔g6 38 ♔xd2 ♔xg5 39 ♖xh2! (protecting the c-pawn) looks quite good for White, e.g. 39...c4 40 bxc4 ♖xb2 41 ♔c3! and the c4-pawn could be a runner. This leaves 36...♔g8, when White does indeed secure the draw by repeating with 37 ♖g7+ ♔h8 38 ♖h7+! etc.

In other examples in this book I have sympathised with a couple of strong players despite their making very poor moves (blunders), but here I am sure that Hungarian GM Zoltan Varga will have been quite annoyed with himself after the game for missing the implications of the kamikaze check on h7. This is because his choice in the game is tantamount to a resignation as the subsequent ending is hopeless for White, and it is not Varga's style to go down without a fight, particularly in this case when he has endeavoured to dictate proceedings since the opening phase. Moreover we have a situation here (in the latest diagram position) where a number of pieces are 'connected' in some way. There is a chain in which Black's king is in check from White's rook, which can be captured by the king on a square that would leave it in another check after the capture of the bishop, which defends the rook, which in turn is attacked by White's king... Such relationships are sure to experience trouble! Imagine being confronted with the position in a magazine or book, with the caption 'White to play...' and a clue that White needs to address the problem of the invading rook. With this prompting, when we are expected to find something flashy (and when we might have just solved many such problems), then ♖h7+ might come easily. But in a game there is nobody to tap us on the shoulder at the critical point to say: 'Have a close look here! All is not lost... use a little lateral thinking' – we can only help ourselves. And this means being sufficiently optimistic to continue looking for problem-like possibilities even when the game seems to be drifting out of our grasp. A club player would be disappointed to not see the wood for the trees in this example, but Varga seems not even to have looked at the trees!

The piece chain, by the way, is worth remembering. While pawn chains stare us in the face, piece chains tend to be hidden or are even waiting to be formed. They are more common than we think. It is not so unusual to see three or more pieces of both colours interlinked, yet time and time again we seem to focus on only part of this chain which, perhaps, might be our only salvation when the situation appears beyond repair, as was the case here.

Stay Focused

We have already seen the young Vallejo Pons let slip a promising bind against Sokolov in their match. Here he has an extra pawn and is well on the way to victory, and in these situations, when the opponent is essentially at your mercy, it pays to keep your eyes peeled for a no-nonsense means with which to finish the game. With the defence already under pressure it is not unusual for this to involve some sort of close quarter combat.

Vallejo Pons-I.Sokolov
Mondariz 2002

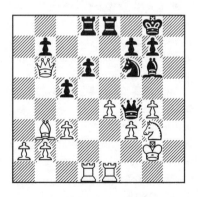

White to move

In the diagram position White has such a possibility (try and find it before reading on...), but instead he grabs another pawn.

27 ♕xb7

More to the point (literally) is 27 e5!, exploiting the pin on the d-file, e.g. 27...♘d7 (27...c4 28 ♗a4) 28 ♕xd6 ♘xe5 29 ♖xe5!

This is not such a difficult position to see, particularly when White chose, instead of e4-e5, to move his queen and should therefore have noticed Black's problem with the rook on d8. And e4-e5 deserves at least to be considered as a candidate. Perhaps White casually took on b7 thinking it effectively ended the game and saw too late what was to come. Whatever he was thinking, it wasn't enough, and he could have saved himself considerable trouble by not relaxing.

27...c4! 28 ♗xc4 ♖b8 29 ♕a7 ♖xb2+

Suddenly Black is back in the game with a rook on the seventh rank, while White's queen is some distance from his not very solid kingside.

30 ♖e2 ♘xg4!

Black strikes while the iron is hot –

otherwise White will consolidate and once again have a comfortable material lead. Compared with the position when we joined the game, when Black was a pawn down with no prospects, he is now happily stripping away at White's defences with a renewed vigour.

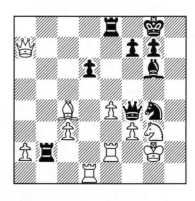

31 fxg4 ♗xe4+ 32 ♔h3 ♖xe2

32...♕h6+ 33 ♘h5.

33 ♗xe2?!

33 ♕xf7+ ♕xf7 34 ♗xf7+ ♔xf7 35 ♘xe2 leaves White a pawn up.

33...♕h6+ 34 ♘h5 and now Black – perhaps because he had not fully adapted to the new situation in front of him – missed 34...♗f5! 35 ♕f2 ♕xh5+

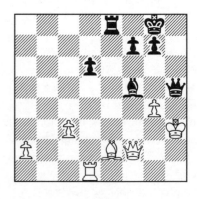

Then 36 ♔g3 ♕g6 might even favour Black.

Instead after **34...♗c2? 35 ♖e1** White was given time to protect his bishop so that now after 35...♗f5 36 ♕f2 Black's only chance would be 36...♖xe2 (36...♕xh5+ 37 ♔g3) 37 ♕xe2 ♕xh5+ 38 ♔g3 ♕g5, when White has 39 ♕e8+ ♔h7 40 ♖h1+ ♔g6 41 ♕e2. In the game **35...♗g6 36 ♕f2 ♕d2 37 ♘f4 ♕xc3+ 38 ♔h2 ♕e5 39 ♔g1 ♗h7 40 ♘g2** left Black with insufficient compensation (1-0, 51).

Winners Never Quit and Quitters Never Win...

So White had a lucky escape thanks to his opponent missing a crucial resource. This example could prove more useful to us as a warning of the dangers of taking the foot off the pedal when the finishing line is in sight than to Vallejo Pons himself, for he won (fairly comfortably, in a way) and might not have been aware of the ...♗f5 possibility until long after the match. When this happens the winner tends to underplay the significance of inaccuracies in near decisive positions, moving on to the next game blissfully unaware of his fallibility. Having said that, I doubt Spain's latest talent got where he is today without going through his games in great detail.

Don't be Stereotyped

Rules are there to be broken! There are countless 'golden' rules. Some we would do well to adhere to as often as possible yet choose – unfortunately – to do so only at our convenience, while others serve as useful guidelines. Throughout this book I have stressed the importance of a player's ability and willingness to appreciate his psychological weaknesses

in order to remain as clear-thinking as possible during a game. While this means becoming used to playing in a logical fashion it does not, of course, preclude having an open mind.

It is not unusual to find oneself in a difficult situation where conventional methods offer no relief. What tends to happen then is that the game continues to be uncomfortable and gradually becomes worse. More versatile players who don't allow their thinking to be shackled by the restraints of convention, and who are not afraid to consider breaking a few rules, perform better under pressure. It is important to make the distinction between sensible, logical play and a rigid, stereotyped approach to chess. A little knowledge can be a dangerous thing, and a lot of knowledge can be very dangerous if we let our horizons be limited by what we have learned. There is none better than Korchnoi to provide a simple example of how defying convention can be the most logical option.

Suetin-Korchnoi
USSR 1967

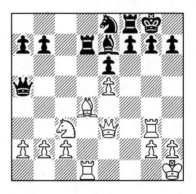

Black to move

Black enjoys a little influence on the queenside with his queen and rook, while over on the kingside he is cramped, with his rook locked in by the passive knight. It is on the kingside where White has a considerable territorial advantage to add to his menacingly posted queen and rook. Looking at the respective pawn layouts, Black has two decent pawn islands to White's three, the e5-pawn creating some inconvenience for Black in that it takes away both d6 and f6 but also a potential weakness as it is isolated. White's bishop is a hold-up piece that does stand in the centre of the arena but is handicapped in some way by the e5-pawn and Black's influence on the d-file. But in the here and now what is Black to do? A waiting policy will see White consolidate the centre and queenside before sending the cavalry over to join the offensive with ♘e4, when both f6 and g5 become available. Black's potential problem with f6 just about rules out ...g7-g6, which is directed against White's rook and makes way for ...♘g7-f5 but leaves f6 without pawn protection and creates another hole on h6. Anyway, as we know, we're not supposed to move the pawns in front of a castled king – that's one of the golden rules...

20...h5!

Be honest – did you consider this paradoxical thrust? Black is in danger of coming under attack on the kingside yet he launches his h-pawn, an act which seems at best risky and worst suicidal in view of who has the room for manoeuvre in this sector. Surely Black's kingside problems have been accentuated by

creating weaknesses. Well, Korchnoi's idea is actually quite logical for (at least) a couple of reasons. The most obvious is new control of g4 in order to deny White's rook(s) access and therefore prevent a doubling on the g-file. From h5 (or h4) the pawn also facilitates the desired occupation of f5 by Black's knight as it prevents eviction with g2-g4. Let's see how the product of Korchnoi's unfettered style fits in with his general strategy.

21 ♖f1 ♕b4 22 ♘e2 ♕c4

A nice square. From here the queen monitors the a6-f1 diagonal (pinning the knight), adds pressure to d4 and hits a couple of queenside pawns. Remember that the kingside is White's domain here as he is not sufficiently represented on the queenside, so he continues as per plan.

23 c3 g6 24 ♖gf3 ♘g7

Here it comes...

25 b3 ♕a6 26 ♘g3 h4 27 ♘e4 ♘f5 28 ♕f4

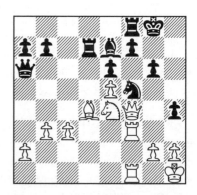

White has been consistent in terms of his kingside play, and Black's own action there has left f6 vulnerable now that the knight has reached e4. However, with the sting taken out of the threat on the g-file and the h4-pawn well protected, Black has succeeded in encroaching upon his opponent's territory, and establishing the knight firmly on f5 (what a transformation considering the terrible posting on e8!) is a further spanner in the works for White because it obstructs the f-file, defends g7 and h6 and has d4, e3 and g3 in its sights. We can conclude, then, that Black has made considerable progress on the kingside thanks to his audacious but entirely logical thrust. In fact Black seems to be doing fine. A key factor here in determining the fate of the game is how the players cope with these latest developments. As the changes have been instigated by Black it is reasonable to assume that Korchnoi, who probably had this position in mind, is more in tune with the state of play.

28...♕xa2 29 ♗c5

Here is an example of the relevance of Black's h-pawn: 29 g4 hxg3 30 hxg3 ♔g7 31 g4 ♖h8+ 32 ♔g1 ♖h4

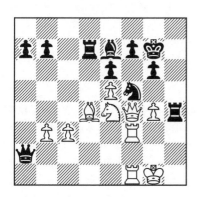

Yet another justification of Korchnoi's battleplan, this time putting Black on the offensive!

29...♕e2 30 ♖3f2

30 ♘f6+ ♗xf6 31 ♗xf8 ♗xe5 is not

possible so White bothers the enemy queen, when the game heads towards a draw.

30...♕d3 31 ♖f3 ♕e2 32 ♖3f2 ♕d3

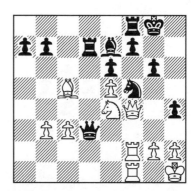

Black has generated enough pressure to counter-balance his earlier problems and settles for a draw. White, however, is not impressed...

33 ♖d2?

Clearly not satisfied with a draw, White turns down the repetition. There is nothing wrong with fighting spirit, but in order to justify playing for the full point White needs to have adapted to the different circumstances brought about by Black's uncompromising expansion – particularly at this level, where a deep overview of what is happening is imperative and mistakes are pounced upon. Korchnoi continued the struggle in style.

33...♕xd2 34 ♘xd2 ♗xc5 35 ♘e4 ♗e3 36 ♘f6+

Hasty but understandable. Preferable is 36 ♕f3, holding back the occupation of f6 until it is more favourable. But by now White was probably somewhat unsettled, having once again been swept along with Black's choice of direction. It is true that White chose to keep the game going with 33 ♖d2, but queen sacrifices tend not to be heavily analysed when alternatives are available.

36...♔g7 37 ♕c4 ♖dd8 38 ♘g4 ♗b6

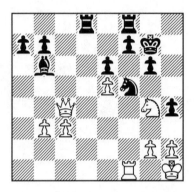

Black has a rook, a powerful bishop and a pawn for the queen. Note how the h4-pawn plays such an important role here, almost bullying White. It is not uncommon in these circumstances for the player with the queen to find himself being outnumbered as more pieces leave the board. Here Black has no problems on the queenside, considerably more influence in the centre and more than enough space on the kingside, but there was not an opportunity to exploit these advantages because White now made another mistake.

39 ♘f2? ♗xf2 40 ♖xf2 ♘e3 0-1

Most players thrown in at the deep end in the initial position would have sat back, without a decent plan, and (most likely) suffered the common fate of being on the wrong side of a strong attack. Many games take this course because the defending side lacks room for manoeuvre, is cramped and is too busy awaiting the inevitable offensive to organise anything approaching counter-play. But this example demonstrates the efficacy of what in many cases are positionally sound, albeit paradoxical responses to threatened aggression. Not only did Korchnoi's seemingly unconventional change of gear prove effective on the board, but the psychological implications were no less significant. The subsequent course of the game suggests that Black's superior appreciation – resulting from his pro-active approach – of developments was in contrast to White's decreasing control and eventual failure to readjust and – equally important – reassess. 'Don't move pawns in front of your (castled) king' is an oft-quoted golden rule, but another, more useful version that I have heard over the years is 'Don't make unnecessary pawn moves in front of your king' – the addition of the word 'unnecessary' makes a crucial difference. The importance of this game cannot be overstressed, for we find ourselves in such cramped positions more often than we would like, and chess is indeed a game so rich in possibilities that 'odd' or conventionally 'incorrect' moves can work out perfectly – both on and off the board.

Passive or Pro-active – Your Choice

We often find ourselves, when slightly worse and under a little pressure, with an interesting choice of either settling for keeping the tenable but unpromising position or seeking to mix it by tempting the opponent with what looks like a concession, usually in the form of an offer of material. Here is such an example contested between a couple of big hitters.

Tal-Petrosian
USSR Championship 1958

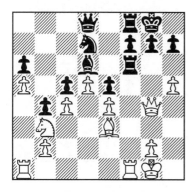

Black to move

White has more space, the superior pawn structure (including a well connected passed pawn), the more useful, active pieces, a target in the form of the backward c5-pawn and pressure on the kingside. In fact White threatens 32 ♗g5, e.g. 32...♖xf1+ 33 ♖xf1 ♕c7 34 ♗h6, or 33...f6 34 ♕e6+, so the obvious move for Black in the diagram position is 31...♔h8. However, this serves only to parry a threat but does nothing else for Black, who would still be left with his cramped, passive pieces and inferior pawn layout, resigned to waiting while White continues to generate further pressure. Instead Black essayed another option designed to exploit his opponent's confident mood, offering an exchange sacrifice that he hoped White would consider a natural by-product of the kingside pressure.

31...♖f4!

Get your retaliation in first...

32 ♗xf4

White accepts the offer, trading in his initiative for a points advantage. This is an understandable reaction when a player is already ahead in some way, coming as a 'reward' for work done. Nevertheless the result of the text is to seriously alter the nature of the game, producing the very imbalance desired by Black. Moreover, with the departure of White's bishop goes much of his control of the dark squares and, in turn, control of the game. Add to this the e5-square about to be available to Black and the opening of the b8-h2 diagonal for the unchallenged bishop, and ♗xf4 begins to look like a doubtful decision. Furthermore, given that we already established that White stood better in the diagram position, then why not make a like-for-like trade on f4 instead, thus preserving the more concrete advantages while netting a pawn in the process? After 32 ♖xf4! exf4 33 ♗xf4 the same pieces remain on the board and Black has insufficient compensation for the pawn, e.g. 33...♘e5 34 ♕g3 ♘xc4 35 e5 or 33...♕f6 34 ♗xd6 ♕xd6 35 ♖f1 etc.

The instructive point here is that White had clearly been on the offensive for preceding dozen or so moves and was therefore on the lookout for some kind of return for his efforts. Consequently he was more willing to take with the bishop rather than the rook on f4 than perhaps would have been the case had he not been pressing so hard. Moreover, White seems also to have viewed ...♖f4 as a symptom of Black's practical, defensive problems – not necessarily forced, but a concession that Black could feasibly be prepared to live with instead of continued pressure from Tal. But this is exactly how Petrosian disguised his cunning plan! Anyway, the game continued:

32...exf4 33 ♘d2 ♘e5 34 ♕xf4 ♘xc4 35 e5 ♘xe5 36 ♘e4 h6

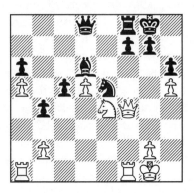

White has parted with a pawn in order to earn himself a decent outpost for his knight, but other features have taken a turn for the worse in the latest diagram position. White's passed pawn, for example, was recently protected on both sides by its neighbours but now it is isolated, while Black's hitherto passive minor pieces suddenly enjoy activity. Meanwhile White all but surrendered his initiative to grab the rook, and now finds himself unable to dictate matters. With this in mind White might have considered 37 ♘xd6 ♕xd6 38 ♖fe1 f6 39 ♖ad1, which at least eliminates Black's transformed bishop. Nevertheless White is still without any pawn breaks with which to open the game and his rooks are sitting pretty with nowhere to go.

37 ♖ae1 ♗b8

An aggressive retreat that is typical of long-range pieces. The threat is a fork on d3, prompting White to admit that his previous move was an error.

38 ♖d1 c4 39 d6 ♘d3 40 ♕g4

♗a7+ 41 ♔h1 f5

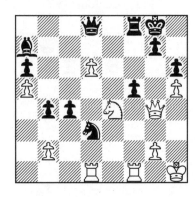

In the space of ten moves the game has undergone a complete transformation, not least thanks to Black's wonderful minor pieces. Note how White's extra rook has been invisible. After **42 ♘f6+ ♔h8 43 ♕xc4 ♘xb2 44 ♕xa6 ♘xd1 45 ♕xa7 ♕xd6 46 ♕d7 ♕xf6 47 ♖xd1 ♖b8** Black emerged with an extra pawn and a firm grip.

Traps

The advice to 'never resign' should not be adhered to too far, of course, but it is precisely in ostensibly hopeless situations that we are occasionally presented with the opportunity to trap an opponent for whom the game has already been won. It is when a lead is so great, when the full point so inevitable, that many players are guilty of assuming a casual air, a feeling of invincibility enveloping them that results in the dropping of barriers and a relaxing of the sense of danger.

'Man is a gaming animal. He must always be trying to get the better in something or other.'
Charles Lamb (1775-1834),
British essayist

Of course such an attitude is completely unjustified while there remain even a couple of enemy pieces in play, yet – once again – not one of us knows a single experienced player whose chess career has not been blighted by an embarrassing reverse in an overwhelmingly winning position. When hoping to set a trap it helps if the opponent has a specific, simple game-winning plan at his disposal. In such circumstances what tends to happen is that the defender will make a token effort to address this plan or to cause a temporary distraction in another sector of the board and, after this inconvenience has been dealt with, the victor will return to finishing off the job. Let us put ourselves in Black's shoes in the following, seemingly helpless position.

Bouaziz-Miles
Riga Interzonal 1979

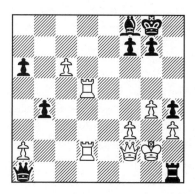

Black to move

White is an exchange up for which Black has absolutely no compensation, the c-pawn is ready to promote and Black's queen and rook are powerless. But Miles decided to continue the struggle nevertheless... Back in 1979 adjournments were used, so this game is all the more interesting as an example of over-confidence when we bear in mind that White even had a break in which to triple-check his (end of game) battle-plan!

42...♖c1 43 ♖c2 ♕b1 44 ♖dd2 ♖h1

Back where it started, but White was threatening to exchange rooks and play ♖c2. By now Bouaziz might even have considered Black's latest to be tantamount to resignation, hence his next.

45 c7?? ♖xh3!!

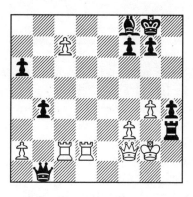

Whatever the result of this sacrifice it is still an obvious possibility and, since it takes place in the heart of White's kingside, requires some level of analysis. Presumably White had put a certain amount of effort and thought into the preceding forty moves, so why not take the time to rule out anything unpleasant that might put the full point in jeopardy? Yet it appears that White failed to give ...♖xh3 the time it deserved in the initial playing session, during the break for the adjournment and even now, before adding the finishing touches by pushing the c-pawn. Hopefully what happens next should serve as a warning against complacency in winning positions, or at least make us aware of our own frailties for when such a scenario next occurs.

46 ♔xh3? ♕h1+ 47 ♕h2 ♕xf3+ 48 ♔xh4 ♗e7+ 49 g5 ♗xg5+ 0-1

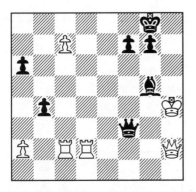

Definitely not the final position White had in mind! The two rooks and future second queen on c7 mean nothing when we look at the opposite flank, where the king is about to be caught after 50 ♔xg5 f6+ 51 ♔h4 g5 mate, or 51 ♔g6 ♕g4 mate.

Returning to the position after 45...♖xh3, more circumspect play from White would have resulted in him salvaging something from the game (not forgetting a welcome dose of pride): 46 ♕f1 ♖g3+ 47 ♔f2 ♖xf3+ 48 ♔xf3 ♕xf1+ 49 ♔e4 and Black must continue to deliver checks. Incidentally, instead of the awful, telegraphed 45 c7?? White could have played, for example, 45 ♖d8, e.g. 45...♖xh3 46 ♔xh3 ♕h1+ 47 ♕h2 ♕xf3+ 48 ♔xh4 and the bishop is pinned, and 48...♕f6+ 49 g5 ♕xd8 50 ♖d2 is final, or 45...♖c1 46 ♖xf8+ ♔xf8 47 ♕c5+ followed by 48 ♖xc1.

A good time to set a trap is when you are already under pressure and your opponent is pressing and expecting to be rewarded for his efforts with some kind of lead. In such a situation, perhaps when faced with an awkward threat, it is not unusual to try to alleviate the pressure with an unsound sacrifice or, equally unsurprising, to simply make a mistake. And we are much less sceptical of favourable opportunities in favourable positions.

Kudrin-Tal
Titograd 1984

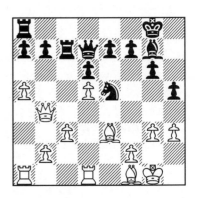

Black to move

White has the bishop pair, more space, exerts pressure on the queenside and threatens to embarrass the knight with f2-f4. Black needs to address this last point.

19...♕f5!

On the face of it this seems only to provide the knight with an escape square on d7. There is certainly nothing to worry about for White as far as the kingside is concerned as Black's pieces are hardly set out to do any damage in this sector. But wasn't the queen doing a specific job on d7 in defending the rook? No doubt Kudrin had already seen and subsequently analysed his next when turning the screw earlier, so apart from checking for unpleasant surprises probably spent little time on what he must have considered a natural product of his positive play.

20 ♗xa7

Setting up an unusual fork should Black recapture.

20...♖xa7! 21 ♕b6 ♘f3+ 22 ♔h1 ♖c4 23 ♕xa7 ♖h4!!

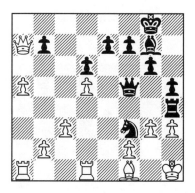

In order to collect his extra material White has both spent time and sent his queen way over to the queenside. Obviously he will have taken this into consideration before going down this route with ♗xa7, but I doubt he found Tal's latest, which the former world champion could well have had up his sleeve when we first joined the game! GM Keith Arkell, when asked about long-range captures that leave a piece cut off from the rest of its forces and far away from the action, responded with a question of his own: 'Would you consider sending a piece into the wilderness without material gain?' – A simple, logical, common-sense piece of advice, perhaps but, like so many of the exam-ples in this book, we tend to allow ourselves the dubious luxury of breaking or altering rules when a nice-looking opportunity presents itself. White's play here has been motivated by the prospect of clearing away Black's queenside, but this leaves him susceptible to attack on the other flank, where there is suddenly a threat of mate beginning with ...♖xh3+ etc.

24 gxh4 ♕f4 25 ♔g2 ♘xh4+ 26 ♔g1 ♘f3+ 27 ♔g2 ♘h4+

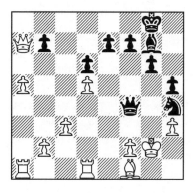

A tidy perpetual check with which to split the point.

Although White could consider himself rather fortunate not to have lost after the disintegration of his kingside he would prefer to return to the initial diagram position and start afresh from there with his long-term advantages intact. We should remind ourselves when in a confident mood and sitting pretty on a promising position that there is rarely an easy route to a clear lead, even if we expect to see our play furnish a concrete advantage in the near future. Doubts about certain aspects of an ostensibly promising line should not be ignored just because something good may well be waiting to be found!

Always expect the unexpected...

Maric-Gligoric
Belgrade 1962

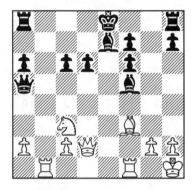

Black to move

A typical, rather messy Sicilian Defence. White threatens the c6-pawn, Black chooses to castle rather than protect it.

17...0-0 18 ♗xc6? ♖ac8 19 ♗b7 ♖xc3! 20 ♖xf5

White will have seen as far as – and will have been satisfied with – this position when setting the ball rolling with the capture on c6. However, before castling Black had seen further...

20...♖b3!! 0-1

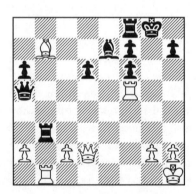

Singing from the Wrong Hymn Sheet

An interesting scenario that is by no means limited to club players is when both players 'expect' the game to follow a specific course and subsequently reach a specific conclusion. It is not unusual to see an important theme (or themes) being evaluated incorrectly on both sides of the board, a 'blindness' that tends to result from one or more stabilising tactics lurking in the background.

The following example is typical.

Kalod-Gross
Prerov 2001

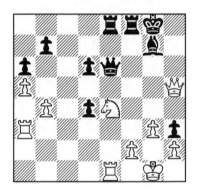

White to move

The 'score' might be level but Black has all but run out of kingside pawns (and light squares), and it is the pin on the e-file that is keeping him in the game. Otherwise White can look forward to an ending in which he can comfortably keep the doubled d-pawns under control while pushing (potentially three!) passed pawns to glory on the kingside. The most accurate move in the diagram position is 29 f3 to bolster the defence of the knight, exploiting the mini-tactic 29...d5 30 ♘f6+, e.g.

30...♖xf6 31 ♕xe8+. White emerges with a clear advantage after 29...♕c4 30 ♖aa1 ♖e5 31 ♕xh3 d5 32 ♘f6+! ♗xf6 33 ♖xe5 ♗xe5 34 ♕e6+ ♔h7 35 ♕xe5. Best for Black is 29...♕c8 30 ♕d5+ ♔h8 with an interesting struggle ahead. Note how ♘f6+, which hits Black hard, has already featured twice in our analysis and a move is yet to be played! No doubt this element led White to practically ignore the potential significance of the pin on the e-file, prompting him to steer the game closer to an ending with his next.

29 ♖f3?? ♖xf3 30 ♕xf3 ♖e7!

Again the hasty 30...d5?? runs into 31 ♘f6+, so Black prepares to attack the knight by leaving the rook protected on e7.

31 ♕h5 d5 32 ♕h7+

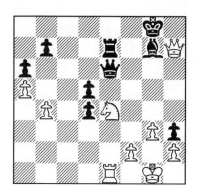

White relies on another tactic to address the situation on the e-file. This time the fork after 32...♔xh7 33 ♘g5+ might well lead to the aforementioned advantageous ending that White has been looking forward to, e.g. 33...♔g6 34 ♖xe6+ ♖xe6 35 ♘xe6 d3? 36 ♘f4+ or 33...♔h6 34 ♖xe6+ ♖xe6 35 ♘xe6 d3 36 ♘xg7 d2 (36...♔xg7 37 ♔f1) 37 ♘f5+ and 38 ♘e3 etc. Best is 33...♔g8

34 ♖xe6 d3 35 ♔f1 ♖xe6 36 ♘xe6 ♗c3, which certainly offers Black more than 35...♖c7?? 36 ♖e8+ ♗f8 37 ♖xf8+ ♔xf8 38 ♘e6+.

32...♔f8 33 f3 dxe4 34 ♖xe4 ♕b3??

For some reason or other – helped along by a combination of the incidental tactics that favour White and White's apparent lack of concern regarding the pin on the knight! – Black now seems to be under the impression that White had matters on the e-file under control all along, culminating in a fresh pin after 34...♗e5 35 ♕h5, when Black's king looks exposed and f3-f4 is coming. It is possible that both players were short of time around this point, as 35...d3 appears to be completely winning for Black. Criticism is easy in hindsight, of course, but after the expected 36 f4 it should not take too long to find the deadly 36...♗d4+!, when 37 ♖xd4 allows mate on e1. However, if we consider the possibilities both played and unplayed thus far, it is quite likely that the protagonists concluded that nothing could be gained for either side on the e-file (ending with the pin on the bishop after 36 f4 seems feasible) and instead concentrated on the ending seen in the game. Ironically this is not uncommon at a reasonably high level (the players' Elo ratings here are approaching 2500), where incidental tactics or a particular motif in a critical line can be enough to send one or both players down a mutually plausible alternative channel – usually one involving simplification. Here, for example, the game seems to be progressing despite the factor of the e-file rather than because of it, neither side believing there to be anything gained there. Moreover this central tension and the players' respect for each other's ability manifests itself in a situation – again not rare at this level – in which both players entertain only the possibility that the 'correct' and logical result is a draw. This can be seen from the manner in which the game ends.

35 ♖xe7 ♕d1+ 36 ♔f2 ♔xe7 37 ♕xg7+ ♔d6

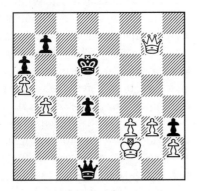

And so we arrive at a queen ending in which the advanced passed d-pawn is a bigger player than White's kingside pawns. Not surprisingly Black's rather exposed king suggests that a draw is there to be found, and White can in fact split the point with 38 g4, e.g. 38...d3 39 ♕d4+, or 38...♕d2+ 39 ♔g3 d3 40 ♕d4+ etc. White's next is also good enough to secure the draw.

38 ♕f6+ ♔d5 39 ♕f5+??

White seems to have been under the impression (at least since we joined the game) that he will not lose and thus sportingly throws in a different check to 39 ♕f7+ ♔d6 40 ♕f6+ with a repetition. Given that the d-pawn is the potential difference between the two sides here – in other words, only Black can

win – it seems illogical and risky not to maintain a status quo when delivering checks. But remember that Black also headed for this drawn ending when a win beckoned...

39...♔c4

Now the king can hide behind the queenside pawns and White's checks are about to dry up.

40 ♕c8+

40 ♕e6+ ♔c3.

40...♔d3?

40...♔b3 leads to a win, e.g. 41 ♕e6+ ♔b2 and the king is safe and the pawn ready to roll (42 ♕e5 ♔b1 etc.).

41 ♕f5+ ♔c4 ½-½

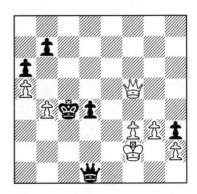

Here, in a position that is winning for Black, a draw was agreed! It is possible that both players had considered nothing other than this result for a while, otherwise White would have stuck rigidly to the correct checks. It is understandable at this point in the game that the queen ending – particularly with Black's queen appearing to be cut off on d1 – points to a perpetual, but there is no excuse for failing to delve a little further. Clearly White has been careless, but I wonder if Black would have been so trusting had his opponent been rated

200 points lower!

Even the annotator sings along in the next example!

A.Horvath-Schenk
Budapest 2001

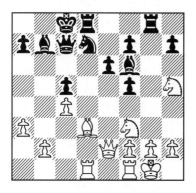

White to move

Black might lack pawn cover for his king but his rook and bishop team up on the g-file and the long diagonal to put White under pressure. Nevertheless White also has a couple of tricks up his sleeve here, prompting Horvath to turn down the safe if slightly passive-looking ♘xf6 followed by dropping the knight back to e1 in favour of active defence.

18 ♗xf5?

The beginning of an attractive but faulty series of captures. But now it is Black's turn to address threats.

18...♕c6!

Accentuating the pressure on g2 and leaving two white pieces en prise in view of the threat to take on f3. The simple 18...exf5 19 ♖xd7 ♖xd7 20 ♘xf6 ♖e7 21 ♕c2 ♗e4! looks like a clear advantage to Black, whose material lead and active pieces should outweigh the scattered pawns.

19 ♖xd7

The point. Finkel awards this a '!' and says that it leads by force to an ending with good winning chances for White. In fact the text is the only follow-up to 18 ♗xf5, as 19 ♘xf6 ♘xf6 20 ♖xd8+ ♔xd8 21 ♗xh7 (21 ♖d1+ ♔c8) 21...♘xh7 22 ♕d3+ ♔e7 23 ♕xh7 runs into 23...♖xg2+

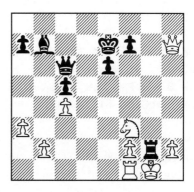

A theme worth storing in your mental 'sense of danger' database!

Back to the game:

19...♕xf3

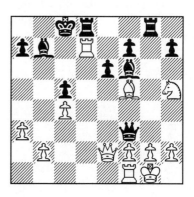

20 ♖xd8+

A complex position! White's king continues to be the focus of unwelcome attention, but Horvath probably thought White was on the way to neutralising the attack. Black seems to have been thinking along the same lines...

20...♗xd8? 21 ♗xe6+! fxe6

21...♔b8 22 ♕xf3 ♗xf3 23 ♘g3.

22 ♕xe6+ ♔c7 23 ♕xg8 ♕xh5 24 ♖e1

Now White had a collection of pawns to go with his rook and, following further progress with

24...♗f6 25 ♕g3+ ♔c8 26 ♕d6 ♕g5 27 g3 ♗d8 28 ♕e6+ ♔c7 29 ♕f7+ ♔c8 30 ♕e6+ ♔c7 31 ♕f7+ ♔c8 32 ♕xh7 ♕g4 33 ♕f7! ♔b8 34 ♕e8 ♔c7 35 ♕e5+ ♔d7 36 ♕e8+ ♔c7 37 ♕f7+ ♔b8 38 b4 ♕h3 39 ♕f4+ ♔c8 40 f3, went on to win on move 58.

So, was this another case of the stronger player skilfully steering the ostensibly troubled ship into calmer, inviting waters? Not exactly. In fact it would be interesting to see whether the game would have taken the same course had the players been sitting on opposite sides of the board. Moreover, not only did Schenk believe his opponent's play, but so did Finkel when annotating the game... If we return to the position after 20 ♖xd8+, it appears that everyone overlooked **20...♔xd8!**.

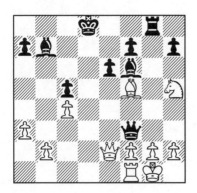

This recapture does look quite odd since it leaves the bishop hanging on f6 and brings the king to the d-file. However, this latter point is the crucial factor because there is no longer time for ♗xe6+, while White is too busy worrying about the g2-pawn to pick up the bishop. Consequently after 21 ♕xf3 ♗xf3 the two black pieces that had the most potential when we joined the game are about to deliver the full point, e.g. 22 g4 ♗xb2 23 ♗d3 (23 ♖b1 exf5 24 ♖xb2 ♖xg4+ 25 ♔f1 ♖xc4) 23...♖xg4+ 24 ♘g3 ♖d4, or 22 ♘g3 exf5 23 gxf3 f4 etc. While ...♔xd8 might not be easy to find in the tense conditions of a tournament, such unlikely moves do tend to receive less consideration when facing a stronger player, particularly a grandmaster. Moreover, when Horvath set off down the path with 18 ♗xf5 the part of the game continuation featuring ♗xe6+, ♕xe6+ and ♕xg8 will have occurred to both players as so natural a transition to some kind of logical new phase that alternatives need hardly be looked for – or even the possibility of their existence entertained!

Yet frustrating the opposition's plans is a key part of chess, and allowing ourselves to go along for the ride just because we have respect for our opponent's ability is a weakness that will be exploited. When facing weaker opposition we often enjoy periods in which we instigate matters, yet when the roles are reversed we don't notice it is happening to us! Here Black seems to have assumed that his attack might have more bark than bite and, consequently, is not surprised to see White wriggle out. One of the reasons why strong players are strong players is an appreciation of this psychological aspect of the game. Uncompromising play, refusing to accommodate a lower rated opponent's desire to steer the game in a specific direction – this kind of approach makes life difficult for the opposition. But such a positive attitude is not exclusive to GMs, of course! Incidentally, it is quite possible that – perhaps short of time – White considered only ...♗xd8, but it is also possible that, being accustomed to not having his bluff called by lower rated players during complicated variations, he deliberately went for this line when contemplating the position in our initial diagram. Like a wily poker player 'representing' a good hand, White might have considered the game continuation with ♗xf5 to be a good practical chance compared with continued passivity (perhaps Black was already short of time...). What is definite, though, is the fact that White's intentions (or lack of them) would have been irrelevant had Black trusted only in himself.

The Danger of the Short Cut

It doesn't matter how we win. In a winning position, the mission is to secure the full point. But who hasn't been guilty of wanting to win the game in style? And what about taking a short-cut to victory?

Horowitz-Pavey
USA 1951

Black is completely winning. An exchange and two pawns up, he will soon add to his collection. White may as well resign. Instead he played...

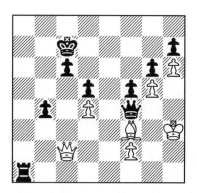

White to move

37 ♕e2

Black decided to tidy up with...

37...♕xf3+??

'Chess is vanity' – Alexander Alekhine.

38 ♕xf3 ♖a3

The convenient expectation is that White will resign now that the liquidation of the major pieces will see the promotion of the b-pawn. Alas, the game ended

39 ♔h4!! ♖xf3 Stalemate

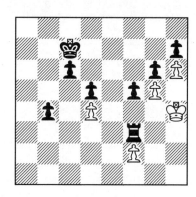

Admit your Mistakes

Despite the fact that nobody is perfect, we don't like to admit our mistakes. Pieces mistakenly placed on inappropriate squares tend to stay there, while we are often guilty of carrying out a particular idea or game-plan once it has begun even though we might feel it is no longer the best course of action. If we change our intentions it might be seen as a weakness or an indication of incompetence to the opponent and – worse – whoever else is watching. We don't want to endure any unnecessary embarrassment during a game... Here is an example of a strong player immediately coming clean and putting practical considerations ahead of his ego.

Rowson-Ellers
Bundesliga 2002

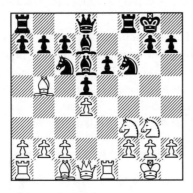

White to move

The two main features of the diagram position in this French Defence scenario are the backward e6-pawn and the related weakness (for Black) on e5, around which we can expect much of the current phase of the game to revolve. In fact White has a pawn, rook and knight all with e5 in their sights, while he is poised to eliminate a key defender of this key square with ♗xc6. However, Scotland's talented GM took

his eye off the ball.

12 ♘g5?!

This does attack the e6-pawn but forcing Black's next might not work to White's advantage. A constructive move is 12 c3 to bolster the centre.

12...♖e8 13 ♘f3!

White has a firm enough grip to claim an advantage here so the wasted time is not of great significance. What is important for us is the fact that Rowson has no reservations about simply returning the knight to f3, re-establishing his control of e5 now that Black has brought his rook to the e-file. Ironically, seeing such a sensible approach from a GM seems quite impressive yet, at the same time, completely natural – after all, 13 ♘f3 is just a move like any other. In fact the effect of this example – I hope – might be to prompt us to wonder why we are so averse to admitting 'mistakes' when, in reality, doing so would appear to be the best, 'professional' thing to do. Anyway, it is worth playing through the next few moves because the knight has its day... **13...a6 14 ♗xc6 bxc6 15 b3 c5 16 dxc5 ♗xc5 17 ♗b2 ♗b4 18 c3 ♗d6 19 c4 c6 20 ♕c2 c5 21 cxd5 exd5 22 ♘g5!** and the knight returned to g5 with a vengeance...

Think for Yourself

Gligoric once wrote: 'It is amazing how frequently players, well informed through computer databases, will automatically copy moves they have seen in other games. A similar readiness to keep playing obvious (but slightly wrong) moves is sometimes shown even by the top grandmasters themselves, so opening inaccuracies may be played for years and years without being noticed.'

After a studying and preparing for a day Gligoric played the following:

Gligoric-Nevednichy
Novi Sad Team Tournament 1999

1 d4 d6 2 e4 ♘f6 3 ♘c3 g6 4 ♘f3 ♗g7 5 ♗e2 0-0 6 0-0 ♘c6 7 d5 ♘b8 8 ♖e1!

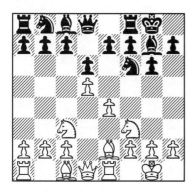

Gligoric: 'Developing as quickly as possible is the only correct approach. This is much better than the most frequently played 8 h3 which wastes a vital tempo for the efficient protection of his newly established stronghold on d5... After all, 8...♗g4 was not a real threat.'

8...c6 9 a4!

Gligoric: 'It is hard to imagine that this normal strategic move (from the exact move order 8 ♖e1, 9 a4) was played only once before in a game Miles-Seirawan, Lone Pine 1976. White captures space on the crucial queenside and threatens to increase his space control even more with 10 a5. Usually White has played 9 h3, going back to the inaccurate plan of earlier competitions, or the equally less efficient 9

♗f1.' The game continued...

9...a5 10 ♘d4! ♖e8 11 ♗f3! ♘fd7 12 ♗e3 ♕c7 13 h3

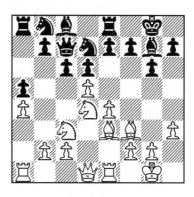

Gligoric: 'Now, with Black's development slowed down, White has time for this useful move, which controls the g4-square.' White has more space, well placed forces and a significant development lead, but the important point to remember here is that his way of dealing with the opening is a result of his *own* preparation. This does not at all mean that we should ignore previous games and stay away from databases, rather that we should not take for granted current theoretical recommendations, even if these are based on many years of international practice. Of course top players have a level of understanding that most of us dream of, but chess is a logical game and, given enough time, we should be capable of producing something along the lines of logical thought! Nothing in Gligoric's thinking is difficult to understand, so there is no reason why the rest of us cannot replicate such reasoning – even during a game, although this is a far more difficult task than in the less urgent context of preparation.

(Im)patience

Nearly all of us feel rather uncomfortable defending, particularly against stronger opposition. The next example features a common reaction. In difficult circumstances we tend to be on the lookout for a way to try to relieve the pressure through a series of exchanges. Of course this is a perfectly natural way of thinking, but the danger is our urge to clear away a few pieces might well prompt us to make matters worse...

Golod-De Vreugt
Lvov 2001

White to move

Black is clearly under a little pressure in the diagram position, with his queenside pawns and e5 vulnerable, White's pieces very actively posted and – last but by no means least – the passed d6-pawn an unwelcome visitor.

24 ♘xf6

It is one thing having a dominating position and another to actually do something about it, so White, satisfied that he has both enough targets (e5, b6 and the related c5) and a possible runner in the shape of the d-pawn, insti-

gates a change. Now 24...♘xf6? runs into trouble after 25 ♘xe5 ♗xa4 26 ♘f7+ ♖xf7 27 ♗xf7, e.g. 27...♕d7 28 ♗c4 b5 29 e5! ♘e8 30 ♕d5 etc.

24...♖xf6 25 ♗xd7 ♗xd7

25...♕xd7? 26 ♘xe5 ♕xd6?? 27 ♘f7+ is part of White's reasoning.

26 ♖d3

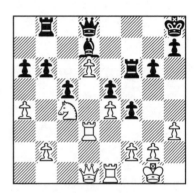

A few pieces might have left the arena but the 'skeleton' of the position is still the same. Unfortunately for Black his remaining minor piece is unable to offer protection to the weak pawns, while the arrival of the rook on the d-file accentuates the danger of the d-pawn. Black's best course now is 26...♖e6 27 ♖d5 ♕f6, keeping an eye on the d-pawn while defending the e-pawn, after which White can claim at least a slight advantage by turning his attention to the queenside with 28 a5.

26...♗xa4?

Of course 26...♖e6 is quite passive and without prospects of counterplay and, consequently, not particularly attractive. Moreover De Vreugt is a young and aggressive player not used to such circumstances. Perhaps this is why Black now results to the following 'simplification' which, unsurprisingly, not only fails to improve his chances but results in greater difficulties.

27 ♕xa4 b5 28 ♕xa6 bxc4 29 ♕xc4 ♖xd6 30 ♖ed1!

Despite being no more tense than earlier parts of the game the diagram position is nevertheless critical. No doubt this is also what Black was aiming for when he instigated the forcing sequence with 27...♗xa4. Black has traded off his weak queenside pawns and even succeeded in netting the d-pawn, which symbolised White's potentially promising lead. However, problems remain on c5 and e5, while White is quicker to assume control of the important d-file. It is this latter feature which is of particular importance because it is new and therefore unlikely to have been considered in much detail by Black when he weighed up the implications of ...♗xa4. At that point he will have concentrated on more fundamental issues such as possible mistakes, captures, tactics etc. With the removal of the d-pawn a major concern Black will have verified that his chances are okay after ...♖xd6 before affording subsequent possibilities even limited attention (remember that a number of pieces/pawns have changed

location or been exchanged since Black contemplated his options after White's 26th move!). But now it is time to take stock of a new scenario in which only major pieces remain to battle it out, and Black should be careful not to relax now that he has achieved his goal in the latest phase of the game. Surprise, surprise – this is easier said than done... Note that 30 ♖d5 ♖xd5 31 exd5 ♕d6 is only slightly worse for Black.

30...♖d4?

Alas the new beginning is accompanied by a natural but poor move. It is understandable that Black does not want to surrender the d-file, but Black's kingside, which has thus far featured little in the players' considerations, is vulnerable, and White is able to exploit this in decisive fashion. A lesser evil is 30...♖xd3 31 ♖xd3 ♕e7 32 ♖d5 ♖b4 33 ♕c3 ♖xe4 34 ♖xc5 ♕d6 35 ♖b5, although White is on the offensive here. However, natural moves leave Black in as much trouble as the text: 30...♖b4? 31 ♕xc5 ♖xd3 32 ♖xd3 is bad, as is 30...♖bb6? 31 ♕xc5 ♖xd3 32 ♖xd3 ♕b8 (32...♕f6 33 ♕c7) 33 ♕e7 etc.

31 ♕xc5!

The point. Having deduced to what extent Black had anticipated various possibilities it is interesting that Golod mentions in his notes to the game that the text and its implications played a part in his analysis on his 26th move! Indeed it is this clear thinking and reassessing that is the key contributory factor to the result of the game. White's undisputed advantage when we joined the game was such that his opponent's range of analysis was more limited due to the immediate and short-term desire to see White's lead neutralised or lessened in some way. It seems that, as far as Black was concerned, anything that looked half decent would be preferable to the initial diagram position, where White had a threatening stance and Black had too many weaknesses. White, on the other hand, had no such worries and was able to analyse less emotionally and more incisively, permitting him to properly evaluate specific positions. This situation of the defender being satisfied with a difficult future position because it appears to be less a cause for concern than the present one is by no means uncommon, and an appreciation of the respective psychological states of the players and the subsequent implications in the decision making process is sure to improve your results, whichever side of the predicament you find yourself in. Now 31...♖xd3 32 ♕xe5+ ♔g8 33 ♖xd3 ♕xd3 34 ♕xb8+ ♔g7 35 ♕e5+! is decisive, so Black tries another approach.

31...♕f6 32 ♖xd4 exd4 33 ♖xd4 ♖e8

Or 33...♖xb2 34 ♕c8+ ♔g7 35 ♖d7+ ♔h6 36 ♕g8 etc.

34 ♕c3

34...h5?

Losing. 34...♖f8 35 ♖d8! ♕xc3 36 ♖xf8+ ♔g7 37 bxc3 is equally hopeless but 34...♔g8 35 ♕c4+ ♔h8 36 ♖d7 prolongs the game.

35 ♖d8! 1-0

Occasionally we find ourselves in a decent position against a stronger player but with very little by way of a plan. If our pieces are already well placed there is nothing wrong with adopting a waiting policy and putting the onus on the opponent to break the status quo if he is to strive for an advantage. The longer 'nothing' happens, the less patient players become, and the more pieces are moved backwards and forwards, the less obvious become the differences between one position and another. Watch how one of Germany's top players self-destructs.

Wahls-Jugelt
German Championship 2001

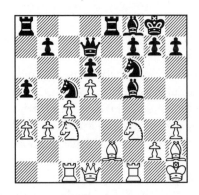

Black to move

The d5-pawn gives White a territorial advantage but the combination of Black's well placed minor pieces and control of the e-file is sufficient compensation. White's FIDE rating is approaching 2600 while Black's is just over 2400, so the underdog begins a 'come and get me' policy in provocative fashion.

20...Ёe3!? 21 Ёf4 Ёee8 22 Ёh2

For the moment White bides his time.

22...Ёe3 23 Ёf4 Ёee8

Draw?

24 ᐃd4

No thanks.

24...Ёg6 25 Ёh2 Ёe3

Here we go again...

26 Ёf4 Ёee8 27 ☖g1 ☖h8!

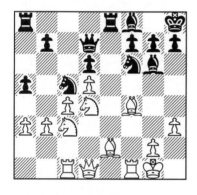

Excellent psychology! The e3-square is no longer available so Black finds another way to irritate his opponent.

28 ᐃcb5 ☖g8 29 Ёc3 ᐃce4

Now that White has ruled out e3 as an entry square Black simply hops into e4!

30 Ёc1 Ёe7

Black certainly seems to be getting the hang of this strategy.

31 ☖h1 Ёf8 32 Ёh2 ᐃc5 33 ☖g1 Ёe4

From the number of moves that have been played it is quite possible that one

or both players could have been short of time here (with the time control likely to have been at move 40). Some strong players are happy to go along with a bit of shadow-boxing at this point in a game, busy looking for ways to suddenly confuse the opponent or waiting to change the nature of the game with the hope of adapting more calmly, of better appreciating any subtle differences that might arise...

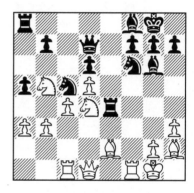

Perhaps White expected yet another visit to e3, when we start all over again – in fact 34...Ёe3 35 ☖h1 then gives us a position identical to the one after Black's 25th move, but with Black to play. Whatever White intended, he didn't get the chance! Incidentally, now was the time to change gear with 34 b4!, exploiting the fact that the attacked knight cannot jump into e4 and therefore getting White's queenside rolling.

34 ᐃc3? Ёxd4!

So the rook *can* leave the e-file!

35 Ёxd4 ᐃxb3 36 Ёb6 ᐃxc1 37 Ёxc1 and Black won a pawn, converting his lead on the 53rd move. Note how it required absolute minimum effort from Black to find himself with a near decisive advantage against a strong

GM – Wahls did the work (what little there was) for him.

Tunnel Vision

It takes only a fraction of a second to find the focal point in our next example.

De Vreugt-Levin
Lvov 2001

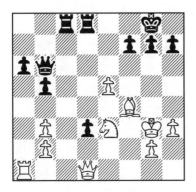

Black to move

White has two pieces for a rook and pawn, which is usually a decent trade. Here, however, Black's major pieces are well posted and the extra pawn is well supported, passed and already on the sixth rank – factors which combine to give Black the advantage. Indeed Black decided to use the d-pawn to reduce his opponent to passivity.

27...d2 28 ♘f1 ♖c6?

Perhaps Black expected a capture on d2 or anyway intended 29...♖g6+ and 30...♕f2 – which White prevents with his next – but Black should have stamped his authority on the game with 28...♕g6+ 29 ♔h2 ♕e4, e.g. 30 ♗xd2 ♕xe5+ and 31...♕xb2 etc.

29 ♕e2 ♖c2

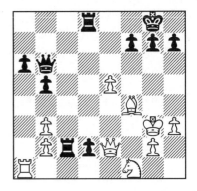

I'm sure this incursion was also part of Black's plan, which clearly revolves around the inconvenience in White's camp generated by the problem d-pawn. While this is a natural strategy on which to concentrate there is a tendency when a single pawn, piece or square is receiving so much attention to become fixated with this special feature at the cost of other aspects of the position. However, in this kind of situation it is the aggressor who is usually the more 'focused' of the two, sometimes being a little too determined to make his trump card tell. On the other hand, the defender, by definition, will usually be reacting to his opponent's play and therefore – while waiting to see what is coming next – has 'spare' time with which to explore other avenues that might have gone unnoticed or at least neglected. Consequently we should try to avoid becoming transfixed by what may well be a considerable plus and major factor in our charge but is nevertheless just one part of the whole. Meanwhile, if your opponent – like Black, here – is seeking to exploit something in particular you will be rewarded for keeping on your toes.

'Winning is not the most important thing; it's the only thing.'
Vince Lombardi (1913-70),
American football coach

30 ♗xd2

It seemed earlier that White might have been on the wrong side of a pin on the d-file but the pin is on his second rank. But the price for this pressure is Black's prize possession, so with careful play White should be able to hold. It would be interesting to know whether both players believed that only White had to pay attention here or if White had an inkling that his opponent might continue to be locked on to the same theme.

30...♕g6+ 31 ♔h2 ♖xb2 32 b4 h6

Compared with when we joined the game the material situation remains the same but Black's extra pawn is now being held up on the queenside. The e5-pawn is less of a target than earlier and White, despite the pin, is beginning to get better organised. Black's latest appears to be a signal that he is providing his king with some breathing space in preparation for activity involving the d8-rook...

33 ♖a3 ♕c2?

As predicted Black throws everything at d2, with the kind of position he was probably aiming for when he opted to push his pawn. Thanks to Black's almost telegraphing his intentions White might have been getting a bit excited here...

34 ♖xa6 ♖xd2?

Consistent. Predictable. Losing.

35 ♘xd2 ♕xd2 36 ♕e4! 1-0

Whoops. Black probably thought that

32...h6 was enough of a contribution to his welfare within his first six ranks, an area of the playing field that seems to have featured very little in his considerations, such was his fixation with his d-pawn and the havoc he thought it was creating on d2.

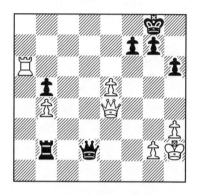

Yet by refraining from executing the check on a8 White has devised his own, decisive theme (mate!), against which there is no decent defence, as 36...g6 runs into 37 e6! etc. What was Black guilty of here? Ironically his tunnel vision aimed exclusively at d2 would have anyway brought no advantage after a queen trade on d2, while the text wins for White. So Black's strategy was flawed almost from the beginning, he insisted on concentrating exclusively on the d-pawn as a pinning theme rather than sending his queen into e4 and he failed to protect his king. He set out on the wrong course and continued to the wrong destination, yet we see this happen all the time and we are guilty of it ourselves. An initiative can so easily drift away, and an advantage can soon be transformed to a disadvantage – both reversals being well within our ability to spoil our own party.

Be Practical

'Do not let what you cannot do interfere with what you can do.'
John Wooden, US basketball coach

Gulko-Timman
Sombor 1974

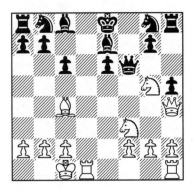

13...b5 14 ♗xb5

Timman – 'I must honestly admit that I had completely overlooked this move; or, to put it less strongly, I had not considered that White would slow his attack to win this pawn. It is easy to understand that, in practice, you do not worry at all about the loss of a pawn when you are in a precarious defensive position fending off an opponent who is a full piece down. It is even one of the principles of defence to return material at the right moment. In this case it occurred unconsciously.'

14...e5

Timman – 'I was not at all shocked by my oversight and played the text move fairly quickly. But not too quickly... a too quick response can be a sign of shock – to your opponent and to yourself.'

Dealing with Odd Situations

Odd situations are difficult enough to decipher with enough time on the clock, but in time trouble the practical problems are accentuated. With the seconds ticking rapidly away – usually as the 40th move approaches – it is vital to keep a clear head and to cut through the complexities. However, a particularly unusual feature in these circumstances suddenly takes on a striking appearance, being almost magnified as the remaining time decreases! The effect can be hypnotic, preventing a psychologically ill-prepared player not only thinking through relevant variations, but even recognising them. Here is a typical example of how a player seeking to secure something definite from an advantage in a 'busy' position can quickly see the game turn against him when confronted with unusual circumstances. Watch how White's efforts to hang onto his lead through retaining the tension culminate in his overlooking an unlikely zwischenzug from his clear thinking opponent.

Kotronias-Atalik
Greek League 2002

In the diagram position White clearly has the upper hand, with a strong passed pawn, more active pieces and a target in Black's vulnerable-looking king. But the open nature of the game, the presence of sufficient heavy pieces, White's own king position and the clock conspire to trouble White. Add to this the fact that, thus far, White has been in the driving seat and has missed a couple of opportunities to edge closer to victory, and we can expect Black to be in a more positive psychological state.

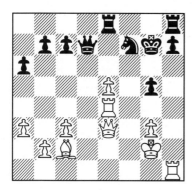

Black to move

37...♕c6!

A nice start, pinning the rook and therefore ruling out the push of the e-pawn in view of ...♖xe6. Consequently one of White's key attacking options has been frustrated and there is the new inconvenience of the now awkward placing of the rook (which hinders the bishop's access to h7) and king. Black even threatens to steal the e-pawn!

38 ♖f1

Intending to meet 38...♖xe5 with 39 ♖xf7+ ♔xf7 40 ♕f3+, breaking the pin and winning after 40...♔e6 41 ♗b3+ ♔d6 42 ♕f6+ etc.

38...♘xe5 39 ♕xg5+

Bringing the rook to the g5-square instead with 39 ♖f5 is another possibility, although after 39...♖hf8 40 ♖xg5+ ♔h8 Black has successfully reorganised his forces, undertaken a threatening stance (the knight is enormous) and the pin remains.

39...♘g6 40 ♕e3! ♖e5!

Perhaps White thought that his next was enough to dissuade Black from the

text, but his opponent is looking to increase his practical chances by notching up the confusion factor. White still has the advantage but its character has altered and the pin is annoying.

41 ♕d4

Setting up a pin of his own.

41...♕d5!

An amazing stand-off, with identical pieces performing identical tasks! With little time in which to properly assess this position – if, indeed, both players managed to anticipate it – Black can only benefit from the unusual development. White might still be a little better on the board but Black has the psychological edge. The trade of queens would steer the game closer to equality while circumstances are not conducive to White's trying to hold on to his lead.

42 ♖f3

Breaking the pin.

42...♖d8

Bringing his final piece into play. White's best is now 43 ♖xe5 ♘xe5 44 ♕xd5 ♖xd5 45 ♗e4!, when both 45...♖d2+ 46 ♔f2 ♖xf2+ 47 ♔xf2 c6 48 b3 (48 ♔e3 ♘c4+ 49 ♔d4 ♘xb2) 48...h6 49 ♔e3 ♔f6 50 ♔d4 b6 51 c4 and 45...♖b5 46 ♔f2 ♘c4 47 ♗d3 ♖c5

48 ♖e2 h5 are a shade preferable for White thanks to the bishop's scope. In this line 45 ♗e4 is far from obvious and White would anyway prefer to keep more pieces on the board. This is the logic behind White's next move, which also frees both rooks. It appears from the ChessBase annotations that the time control has yet to be reached, so it is possible that White also wanted to put the onus on his opponent to make a decision as to where the game should go next. Black did exactly this...

43 ♔f2??

A terrible blunder.

43...♕xe4!

No doubt White was ready only for the capture on d4.

44 ♕xe4

Forced.

44...♖d2+

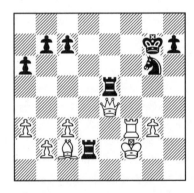

The point behind this crafty check is that 45 ♔e3?? permits 45...♖xc2. Thus after **45 ♔f1 ♖xe4 46 ♗xe4 ♖xb2 47 ♖d3 ♘e5! 48 ♖d5 ♔f6 49 ♗xh7 ♖b3** Black assumed the advantage, which was eventually converted on the 67th move.

White clearly failed to cope with the combination of an unsteady advantage,

a shortage of time and mounting tension in the middle of the arena. Black, on the other hand, having already come to terms with the fact that he stood worse, welcomed the possibility of 'mixing it' – a situation which presented itself quite naturally but nevertheless required a little in the way of direction.

Tricky players enjoy steering the game into murky waters, putting pieces on strange squares, unsettling the opponent. But how do we cope when something bizarre happens? And do we pass over certain possibilities because at the end of a variation we find that one or more of our pieces is embarrassingly placed or looks too odd to be a feasible option? Here is a rather strange example that deserves our attention in terms of how we would conduct the game from either side of the board. We join the game well before the unusual situation arises in order to get a better flavour of the complexities of the struggle.

Volokitin-Firman
Lvov 2001

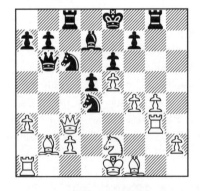

Black to move

The French Defence with 3 ♘c3 ♝b4 typically produces tense early middlegames in which neither king can castle and tactics abound. Black's next is crying out to be played.

17...♘b4!

Seeking to exploit the awkward placing of White's queen.

18 ♘xd4

18 ♕xc8+ ♝xc8 19 ♘xd4 ♘xc2+ 20 ♘xc2 ♕xb2 21 ♝d3 ♝d7 clearly favours Black.

18...♖xc3 19 ♝xc3 ♘a2!

Did you see that one coming?

20 ♝d2

20 ♖xa2 ♕b1+.

20...♕xd4 21 ♖xa2 a6

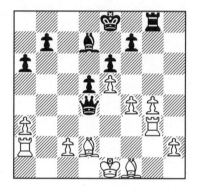

Psakhis assesses this position as slightly better for Black but by no means easy to make something of the advantage. These situations of material imbalance – particularly cases where only one queen remains on the board – are notoriously tricky as the possibilities tend to be varied and evaluations might need to be 'updated' constantly. The power of the queen, of course, is accentuated and therefore especially difficult for the opposition to keep under control...

22 ♝e3 ♕c3+ 23 ♝d2 ♕d4 24 ♝e3

Which kind of player are you? Sitting on Black's side of the board, would you be satisfied – relieved, even – with a draw here because the situation is complicated (and you're more worried about the fate of the queen rather than what damage it can do), or would you prefer to keep the going because the situation is complicated? Confidence can be an important factor, of course, but for this game, at least, Firman fell into the latter category.

24...♕e4 25 ♝d3

Forcing the queen into the corner. An alternative is 25 ♖b2!?, intending to meet 25...d4? with 26 ♝g2, when White stands clearly better.

25...♕h1+ 26 ♝g1 ♖h8 27 c3

27 ♖b2 ♖xh2 28 ♖xb7 ♝b5 helps Black.

27...♝b5!

Black takes the opportunity to trade his traditionally poor French bishop, although 27...♝a4!? 28 ♖b2 b5 29 f5 ♚d7 looks a shade better for Black.

28 ♝xb5+ axb5 29 ♖ag2!

Very odd indeed! Is it possible that one or both players anticipated this bizarre position before Black refused to repeat moves with 24...♕e4 and, if so, who made the correct evaluation in advance? Even now, having arrived here, it is difficult to assess! White has a rook, bishop and pawn for the queen but is using his forces to deny his opponent's most dangerous piece a single square. But who can make progress, and how? Perhaps a good pointer is the fact that Black's rook remains free to make an impact on the game, and White might be too busy 'containing' his opponent to consider more aggressive options.

29...♔d7! 30 f5

Preparing to shore up the queenside in anticipation of the rook's arrival on a8 seems like a good idea at first but, after 30 ♔e2 ♖a8 31 ♗c5 b6! 32 ♗b4 Black simply returns his rook to h8, when the h-pawn is doomed. At least with the text White endeavours to create something (a passed pawn) in the vicinity of his forces.

30...♖a8 31 f6 ♖xa3 32 g5

Black is faster after 32 ♔f2 d4! 33 cxd4 b4 etc.

32...♖xc3!

Exploiting the responsibility of White's pieces by expanding the area in which the battle takes place, clearing away White's queenside in the process. Now 33 ♖g4 ♖e3+ 34 ♔d2 (34 ♖e2 ♕f3!) 34...♖xe5 35 g6 fxg6 36 ♖f2 ♖f5 wins for Black, so White sends his king to carry out guard duty.

33 ♔f2 ♖xg3 34 ♔xg3

Still odd! The cage is still closed on the kingside but matters have altered drastically on the other flank, with Black being the first to create passed pawns. Consequently the situation is much easier to gauge now, for White is unable to operate on both sides of the board.

34...b4 35 ♔h3

Or 35 g6 fxg6 36 ♔f2 b3 37 ♖g4 b2 38 ♖b4 ♕e4!

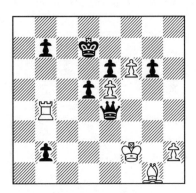

Suddenly the queen springs to life with deadly effect. In the game Black's queen re-entered the game in similar fashion.

35...b3 36 g6

36 ♔g3 fails to 36...♕xg2+ 37 ♔xg2 b2 etc.

36...fxg6 37 f7 ♔e7 38 ♖f2 ♔f8 39 ♖f1

Threatening a nasty check on c5...

39...d4!

Avoiding disaster and winning easily. The game ended:

40 ♔g3 b2 41 ♖b1 ♕c6

41...♕e4 42 ♖xb2 ♕xe5+ is also possible.

42 ♗xd4 ♕c2 43 ♖xb2 ♕d3+ 0-1

Trying to tame a lone queen can be a surprisingly complicated and futile process, particularly when other – even ostensibly minor – problem areas need addressing. When the collective force employed in 'dominating' the queen is of greater 'points' value than the queen itself, then expect something to give somewhere else. Anyway, it is the way the respective evaluations and decisions were made regarding the implications of the trapped queen that we are interested in here, and Black's no-nonsense performance is straightforward, calm, ruthless and instructive. For a while the queen had the least scope of anything on the board (!) but Black's patience and ability to appreciate the full picture was deservedly rewarded.

Déjà Vu

Intuition is a funny thing. The stronger the players whose games we study, the more we trust their intuition. Fantastic games in books and magazines seem almost normal if the product of a super-GM, but most average players have little faith in their own intuition, as successive attempts to follow a 'gut' feeling continue to come unstuck. However, intuition is not the result of a magic wand that can be used only when a game becomes complex and exciting, when a crucial decision has to be made. In fact it comes into play most in mundane, completely normal positions in which we might be required to choose between two or more feasible continuations.

While it is quite likely that top players do indeed possess a more readily accessible and accurate magic lamp from which an intuition genie grants seemingly endless wishes, it is worth entertaining the possibility that more experienced, hard-working, thinking players tend to have a better intuition than lesser experienced, lazy, non-thinkers!

We could discuss the extent of the existence of natural, inborn intuition until the cows come home, but there is no denying the impact of study and experience on a player's ability to navigate his way through 'new' situations.

A resource or useful motif worth remembering has a good chance of being forgotten for years but, when a related scenario next appears in front of us, there is a chance the original will spring from the subconscious and on to the board. Therefore when studying any aspect of chess we should do just that – study. If your typical study session (assuming you have them) involves skimming through twenty moves of theory, then you are on to a loser – your chess vocabulary will simply be too limited, your petrol tank will empty too early, your cupboard will be bare... To get the most from your chess you need to broaden your chess horizons to the maximum, your sphere of experience should be all-encompassing. And this can be done only by giving everything you encounter the consideration it deserves. For example if you allow the logic or reasoning of why playing ...♖fd8 is preferable to ...♖fe8 in certain positions pass you by, then such useful information will fail to take its rightful place in your memory banks. And if it is not there you cannot use it. In his fascinating book *Chess: The Search for the Mona Lisa* the jovial GM Eduard Gufeld recounted two games which were linked in quite remarkable fashion. The following diagram features a critical position from the first game:

Geller-Gufeld
USSR Championship, Tbilisi 1959

Black to play

White has just played 35 ♖e5, placing both rooks on the bishop's diagonal. Not only is it clear that Black is unable to accept this offer due to the exposed nature of his kingside, but it is not clear how Black can defend...

35...♕b2!!

Ironically forcing White's anyway planned assault on the king.

36 ♘f6+ ♗xf6 37 ♖g4+

Now Black's best is 37...♗g7!! 38 ♕f6 ♕b1+ 39 ♔h2 ♕h7 40 ♖e7 ♔h8! and Black is a piece up. Instead Black's attention was to drawn to an inaccurate but spectacular possibility.

37...♗g5? 38 ♖xg5+

The game ended **38...hxg5 39 ♕xg5+ ♔h7 40 ♕h5+ ♔g8 41**

♕g5+ (41 ♖g5+ ♕g7!) with a draw, but Gufeld points out the line 38 ♕xg5+ hxg5 39 ♖exg5+ ♕g7!!

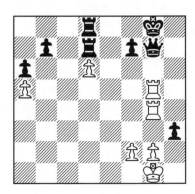

This is the first time I have seen such a situation, as was the case with Gufeld, who noticed that after 40 ♖xg7+ ♔h8 there is no mate, while the double rook ending holds drawing chances for Black. In his notes to the game Gufeld mentions that he didn't know whether Geller had seen this variation.

This is significant because, six years later, the same players reached the following position:

Geller-Gufeld
USSR Army Team Championship 1965

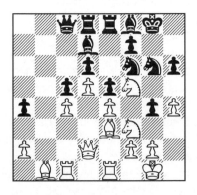

White to move

Again White has the upper hand, and he essayed a piece sacrifice designed to maintain the momentum of his initiative.

27 ♗xh6?! ♘xe4!? 28 ♗xe4 ♗xf5 29 ♘h2 ♗xe4 30 ♖xe4 f5! 31 ♕g5 ♔h7 32 h5 ♘h8

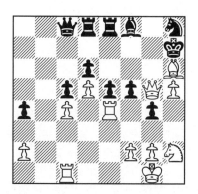

Gufeld: 'Here I thought that I had outwitted the grandmaster because the avalanche of pawns in the centre provides Black with counterplay, whereas White's threats seem to have evaporated. But at this moment Geller found a terrific blow which I had overlooked.'

33 ♖b1! ♗xh6 34 ♖b7+!! ♕xb7 35 ♕xf5+ ♔g8 36 ♖xg4+

Gufeld: 'It seems there is no satisfactory defence. The only plausible-looking reply, 36...♗g7, will be refuted by 37 h6! threatening mate on h7. but while thinking about my 33rd move I had seen the way to salvation! My memory helped me find the 6-year-old move which I now triumphantly demonstrated...'

36...♕g7!!

Gufeld: 'The move which I didn't have the chance to play before! This time, I was lucky enough to play it just when lots of people were standing round our chess table waiting for my resignation. If I hadn't remembered that other game and this special resource, I would not have found the defence.'

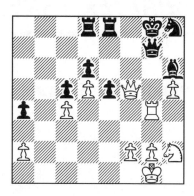

37 ♖xg7+

The game now ended **37...♔xg7** (37...♗xg7 38 ♘g4) **38 ♕g4+ ♔h7 39 ♕e4+ ♔g7 40 ♕g4+ ♔h7 41 ♕e4+ ½-½**

Another perpetual check, with White's queen, ending on the 41st move! The same events with the same players... I wonder if the fact that Gufeld just happened to be facing the same opponent contributed to his finding ...♕g7 a second time? Some psychologists would argue that Geller being the opponent again served as a 'cue' in retrieving the possibility. Nevertheless, had Gufeld not made an effort to 'think chess' in 1959 the same resource probably wouldn't have been available six years later.

Perhaps something in a game you play next week might come in handy in ten years' time! Hopefully some of the material in this book should stay with you for even longer...

Happy thinking!

CHAPTER THREE

Illustrative Games

Space

Pressure comes in many guises. We usually associate being under pressure with being on the wrong side of a dangerous attack, lines opening up against our king, trying against the odds to protect a weak pawn (or weak square) and so on. While these situations can be unpleasant for the defender, as we have seen, they at least feature an agenda that helps in the decision making process – if a wave of pawns is rushing towards your king, for example, the task in front of you is a rather obvious, albeit unenviable one. On the other hand, a situation in which there are no direct threats to contend with or no obvious weaknesses under attack can make life considerably difficult even for strong players if there is little room in which to manoeuvre. This is why a space advantage is so important (all other factors being equal), and in the next illustrative game we will investigate – from both sides of the board – possible implications of extra space.

Some club players are content to give their opponent more space, waiting patiently in a cramped but ostensibly solid set-up, assuming a come-and-get-me stance with the aim of either holding on for the draw or of tempting the opposition into overplaying his hand. Although this is not a fantastic strategy it is nevertheless a surprisingly popular one, and much depends on psychology.

Over the years I have seen many players – from beginner to expert – who become nervous when they find themselves with more than the usual share of territory. This is another surprisingly common problem. The more overwhelming the space advantage, the more overwhelmed the player! You are not alone – particularly if confidence is low for whatever reason – if when you see all this extra room you begin to worry that there are lots of 'holes' that can be exploited by your opponent if you manage to somehow allow him inroads or if you misplay the game to such an extent that an invasion might leave you defenceless, often with no pawn protection as expansion is usually part of the initial territorial gain. Nor is it that rare even on a good day to feel uncomfortable with 'too much' space – such players believe that being in control of the game is down to them rather than being determined by the geometry of the playing area. Generally, however, most of us do appreciate the potential of extra space and, consequently, we are able to weigh up the pros and cons to conclude that it is a luxury worth having (worth working for). More space means more freedom and therefore more control, thus affording us the capacity to translate the original advantage into something tangible.

Once we have established the effectiveness of a space advantage, the convenience it confers and the resulting air of confidence it creates, we can return to the defender's plight. As I said in the introduction to this section, cramped quarters can severely hinder operations. A lack of space tends to accentuate the almost inevitable defensive task, damage a player's confidence and – not surprisingly – in turn lead to below-par decision making. Whatever our fears regarding 'too much' space, we have all found ourselves with nowhere near what we need enough times to appreciate the psychological strain this can cause. In the following game White's treatment of his space advantage is both apparently simple and instructive.

Shirov-Leko
Ljubljana 1995
Ruy Lopez

1 e4 e5 2 ♘f3 ♘c6 3 ♗b5 a6 4 ♗a4 ♘f6 5 0-0 ♗e7 6 ♖e1 b5 7 ♗b3 d6 8 c3 0-0 9 h3 ♘b8 10 d4 ♘bd7

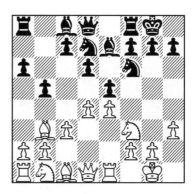

The diagram position has been seen countless times at all levels. By relocating his queen's knight to d7 Black confirms that he aims to concentrate on what he intends to be a strongpoint on e5 which, combined with the early queenside expansion, should provide the second player with some kind of foothold. This is not a very ambitious game-plan but it is in keeping with Leko's style at the time.

Sitting on White's side of the board, of course, is Shirov, one of the most enterprising, aggressive and 'unsolid' players of the modern game, so such a policy might also have been designed to test the Latvian's patience...

11 ♘bd2 ♗b7 12 ♗c2 ♖e8 13 a4

White exploits the fact that ...bxa4 leaves a long-term weakness in the shape of the isolated a-pawn to stake a claim of his own on the queenside. In fact this is the beginning of Shirov's strategy.

13...♗f8 14 b4 ♘b6

Hindsight – as always – is a useful tool but, given what happens in the game, this does seem to be a rather odd choice. However, the text is consistent with Leko's approach, and suggests that he is quite willing to sit and wait for his opponent to act. Such a confident attitude is not for everyone.

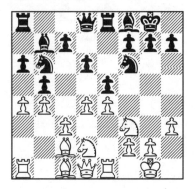

15 a5 ᐧbd7 16 ᐧb2 ᐧb8 17 ᐧb1

The logic behind these mysterious rook moves will soon become clear!

17...h6 18 ᐧa1 ᐧa8

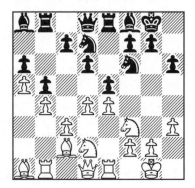

'Shadow-boxing' is often used to describe a sequence of moves such as this, but that suggests that not much is happening. In fact by posting bishops on the long diagonals the players are monitoring e5 (and d4) and e4 (and d5) respectively. Note that White's dark-squared bishop appears to be closed in compared with the bishop on a8, but it actually serves as a deterrent to ...exd4 (hitting the already well protected e4-

pawn – no accident, this!) in view of the increased power of the bishop on the a1-h8 diagonal and – after a future e4-e5 – the implications of the influence of the other bishop on the b1-h7 diagonal. Meanwhile White will soon be ready to further the scope of the bishop anyway with c3-c4, which will bring a fifth white pawn as far as the fourth rank. Then the b4-pawn could come under attack after ...bxc4, which is why Black threw in ...ᐧb8 and ...ᐧa8, and why White responded with ᐧb1 and ᐧa1!. We tend to consider such ideas as exclusive to top players but they are in fact quite logical and not too difficult to arrive at if we approach the game with a clear mind and an appreciation of the plans available to both sides. Because ...exd4 is not an option for the moment Black continues with his modest plan.

19 ᐧe3

Another odd-looking move that is entirely logical. White prepares to strengthen his grip on e4 by putting his queen and rook the correct way round. The third rank also offers the rook some flexibility, as we will see.

19...g6

Preparing to give the bishop a new outpost on g7. Also possible is 19...ᐧh7!? when Black might seek to ease his defensive task a little by trading a pair of knights on g5.

20 ᐧe2

A new move at the time. 20 c4 had been played previously, but Shirov holds fire for a move.

20...c6

Shirov gives 20...ᐧg7 21 d5 c6 as equal. It is interesting that Leko voluntarily places his pawn on c6 (obstructing the bishop) before White has provided him with something to challenge on d5. However, the text is consistent with Black's strategy thus far, albeit a rather committal way of execution in that White has been given a free look at the layout on the queenside. Even from one of the world's top GMs Black's rather negative approach – which effectively replaces what could have been a useful move with an unnecessary and perhaps irrelevant one – seems suspect from a psychological viewpoint. White is simply being given too much freedom as well as an indication as to what Black will do next. Despite the fact that Black is still in a position to maintain the balance, the signs are that he will indeed allow White to dictate matters.

21 c4

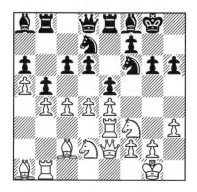

As I mentioned earlier there are players who would feel less comfortable on White's side of the board in the diagram position. The wave of pawns flowing forward can create the impression that potential enemy entry points are being left behind, that White's army is in danger of advancing almost out of his reach, beyond the point of control. But in reality such a concern is rarely justi-

fied, being associated with a lack of confidence. There are many hidden demons waiting for us in every game but, unless one manifests itself on the board, right in front of our eyes, then we should remain confident in both our ability and the actual position. Allowing ourselves to be afraid of unpleasant possibilities that we can neither see nor visualise might be an unfortunately common by-product of human nature but it is also a joyless and restrictive way to play chess.

Looking at the diagram position here on the printed page, sitting comfortably in the living room or at the chess club, it is clear that White enjoys a slight pull thanks to his extra space, while Black – if anyone – might have something to worry about. Yet Leko continues in the same vein...

21...♗g7?

After this there is no going back. Responding to the build-up of tension in the centre rather than ignoring it is preferable. 21...bxc4 22 dxe5 favours White in view of the pawns left behind on a6 and c6, but according to Shirov Black can secure equality with 21...exd4! 22 ♗xd4 bxc4 23 ♘xc4 d5.

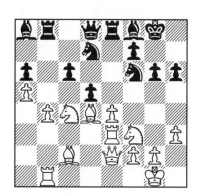

While this is typical of what can happen in the middle of the arena when a number of pawns are involved in a stand-off, Black seems to have had no intention of contributing to the game with an injection of pace. Remember that we are discussing here the implications for both players when someone has a considerable advantage in space. Most players try to avoid cramped positions, and some don't, but the fact that Leko's willingness to curl up in a ball and wait to be kicked is so clinically punished is significant. Lesser players fear these situations – and they are right to do so.

22 dxe5 dxe5 23 c5

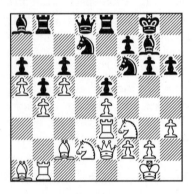

This is exactly what White would have been happy with when he first sent his queenside pawns down the board, and perhaps Shirov was pleasantly surprised to see his opponent help with the construction of the queenside structure we now see with ...c7-c6.

You might have anticipated this position a few moves ago, or even earlier. The situation appears fairly even on the kingside, but on the opposite flank the fixed pawns afford White much more room for manoeuvre. The a1–bishop now enjoys a clear view of the e5-pawn whereas the diagonal of the a8-bishop runs to a total of two squares! In terms of finding squares for his pieces White has at his disposal a block of eight squares on his second and third ranks, while Black is limited to just the four from a7 to d7 (the d6-square belongs to White).

Another consequence of the territorial supremacy is Black's reduced capability to contest the d-file. Overall it is fair to say that Black, without prospects by way of decent counterplay, stands clearly worse. It is also safe to assume that the vast majority of players would jump at the opportunity to play on White's side of the board here, and run a mile from Black's! From White's point of view the trick is to be prepared to simply go with the flow (your flow). This usually involves a certain amount of tension along the way, characterised by the existence of clearance possibilities that have to be weighed up, and the ultimate aim of establishing a situation such as the one we have here. The expansion might seem 'loose' but the increasing space advantage in itself should be enough to make its exploitation by the opposition problematic. This is assuming, of course, that the game is handled with a degree of care and attention.

23...♘h5?!

Already Black starts to go wrong, looking to the kingside for respite instead of addressing his problems with 23...♗b7 24 ♖d3 ♕c7, when he is quite a bit worse but at least improving his pieces and removing the queen from the potentially hazardous d-file.

24 g3 ♕c7 25 ♖d3! ♖bd8

25...♘f8 26 ♘f1 ♘e6 27 ♖d6 with a clear advantage to White according to Shirov.

26 ♖d1 ♘f8 27 ♘f1 ♖xd3 28 ♕xd3

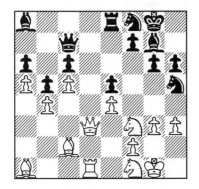

Thanks to the flexible ♖e3 earlier White has been able to make the most of the d-file. Shirov's tendency to create unnecessary complications in favourable positions has more than occasionally led to his downfall, but here the closed queenside and reasonably normal kingside in a way restrict him to a more sober approach. White's plus is his space advantage, which he must nurture in order to keep Black under pressure.

28...♘f6

Black brings his knight back into the fold. Shirov gives 28...♕c8 29 ♔h2 as being decisive.

29 ♘e3 ♗b7 30 ♔g2

Shirov patiently ties up a loose end before accentuating his lead by putting the extra territory to good use. Without the possibility of hitting the h3-pawn Black really is struggling. Playing through the game now it is difficult to imagine what Black was expecting from his game-plan. By now it is evident that the combination of negative factors is becoming increasingly problematic for the defender, so whatever confidence was there earlier has now gone.

30...♕b8 31 ♗b2 ♕c7 32 ♗b3 ♖e7?!

The fact that Shirov recommends 32...♕b8 is indicative of Black's plight. Then 33 ♘g4!? ♘xg4 34 hxg4 keeps Black under wraps.

33 ♕d8!

White's patience and display of controlled play is rewarded. Leko gives 33 ♕d6 ♘xe4 34 ♕xc7 ♖xc7 35 ♗xe5 ♖d7! when White can stay well on top with 36 ♖e1 but at least Black has some freedom.

33...♕xd8

Black has failed to deliver a single blow throughout the game but here there was an opportunity to do so in 33...♘xe4 when Shirov had ready the following: 34 ♘g4! ♖d7 (34...♕xd8 35 ♖xd8 ♖d7 36 ♖b8!) 35 ♕xc7 ♖xc7 36 ♗xe5 ♖d7 37 ♖e1 ♘d2 38 ♘xd2 ♖xd2 39 ♘f6+ ♗xf6 40 ♗xf6 ♖d3 (40...♗c8 41 ♖e7) 41 ♖e8

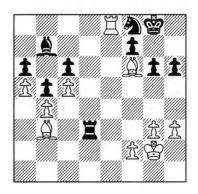

Black's bishop doesn't look too healthy... 41...♖xb3 42 ♗e7 ♖d3 (42...♖xb4 43 ♖xf8+ ♔g7 44 ♖b8) 43 ♗xf8 etc.

34 Rxd8 Ne6d7

34...Rd7 35 Rb8 will soon spell the end for Black, e.g. 35...Nxe4 36 Ng4 Rc7 37 Ngxe5 Bc8 38 Bxf7+ Kh7 39 Be8 etc.

35 Nh4!

Now even the g6-square comes under fire.

35...Kh7 36 Nhf5

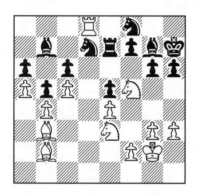

The logical culmination of Shirov's treatment has resulted in a decisive advantage. The compact nature of Black's set-up is illusory; something had to give.

The game continued:

36...gxf5 37 Nxf5 Bf6 38 Nxe7 Bxe7 39 Re8 Bg5 40 Bxf7 Kg7 41 Bb3 Bf6 42 f4 Ng6 43 f5 Ngf8 44 h4 Kh7

Now Black is reduced to passivity on the other flank.

45 Kh3 Kg7 46 g4 Kh7 47 Bc1 Bg7 48 g5 hxg5 49 hxg5 Kh8 1-0

This game served as a good illustration of how an accumulation of space can be deadly – and in such an unassuming fashion! The pressure is subtle rather than obvious, to such an extent that an advantage can reach decisive proportions almost before the victim notices.

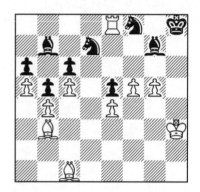

As long as the player in possession of the greater space properly utilises the advantage this confers, a meaningful conversion of some kind is almost inevitable in many cases. Nevertheless, I cannot stress enough the importance of patience in these situations...

Too Much Space...

The nature of a territorial superiority is such that the extra squares made available could very well become irrelevant. Wholesale exchanges might cancel out any hitherto troublesome pressure for the defender and lead to equality. Worse still – these bonus squares could be the cause of serious problems should the opposition find (or be presented with) a way into what is basically a larger target area than usual. In contrast, a lead of an extra pawn, for example, remains intact – all other factors being equal.

Just as defending cramped positions can feel powerless and restrictive, many players' eagerness to serve up this kind of discomfort to the opposition leads them to overplay a space advantage. Earlier I mentioned the negative, fearful approach of over-cautious players who treat extra space like a hot potato, afraid to push too far and get their fingers burnt. But this group of careful individuals will point to others who see even the hint of a bit more room, the possibility to throw their weight around and push the opposition back, as a guaranteed route to an initiative. Such over-confidence is risky indeed, particularly when the mere facility to push pawns becomes the focus of attention at the expense of more important factors. We should approach any stage of the game with a certain level of circumspection, yet the near automatic translation of more space into a 'must-be' advantage is a very common fault in chess. A pawn is a pawn. A weak square in the heart of enemy territory that can be used as a killer outpost is obviously important, a crushing kingside attack is a potential game winner etc. But more space is not necessarily the final, victorious frontier... Handle with care.

The Dangers of Passive Play

We have seen the effects of a space advantage when the protagonists are of roughly equal strength, but when the lead is in the hands of the stronger player it can be lethal with what seems like minimal effort. Even with a considerable disparity in ratings a certain amount of patience is required. We have already discussed the importance of patience in these pages, and this is perhaps of more relevance in this situation – where overplaying your hand can easily backfire – than many other scenarios.

Watch how Khalifman calmly maintains his centre and extra space on the queenside to gradually assume complete control against an opponent whose approach is too passive.

Khalifman-Sivokho
St Petersburg 1996
Queen's Indian Defence

1 d4 ♘f6 2 ♘f3 e6 3 c4 b6 4 ♘c3 ♗b7 5 a3

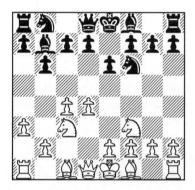

The purpose of the unassuming text might be to rule out the potentially annoying pin after ...♗b4 but Black can soon drift into a lifeless position if he continues with outwardly natural but inadequate play.

5...d5

It would be easy after a2-a3 to settle for 5...♗e7?! and castling and so on, but then with 6 d5 White stakes an early claim to enemy territory, effectively closing out the b7-bishop, keeping Black's centre pawns at bay and preparing to accentuate the space advantage with e2-e4. Even the a3-pawn will soon play a role when White is ready to further expand on the queenside with b2-b4.

This position is reached countless times at club level, Black often coming off worse after struggling in a cramped opening and throughout the middlegame. A friend of mine whose FIDE rating is around the 2200 mark has had tremendous success with a2-a3 lines against the Queen's Indian. A genuine chess thinker, his appreciation of the fact that extra space does not have to furnish its owner with a dangerous attack or initiative for it to be a powerful tool tends not to be shared by the opposition. In most cases his opponents fail to recognise the cause of their downfall when it has actually been staring them in the face since White's pawn landed safely on d5, the 'losing' process being gradual and hardly noticeable to the stereotyped eye.

6 cxd5 ♘xd5

The surest way to maintain a presence in the centre is to recapture with the pawn here, but some players prefer not to voluntarily obstruct the bishop. Of course this is down to taste, as is White's response, which might be ♗f4/g5 followed by e2-e3 or a kingside fianchetto. Sivokho's choice keeps the position more fluid, which is a decent approach against stronger opposition, keeping them on their toes and not providing them with fixed targets on which to focus.

7 e3 g6

Also seen is 7...♗e7, when Ribli-Hort, European Club Cup 1991 continued 8 ♗b5+ (a typical 'spoiler' in these lines) 8...c6 9 ♗d3 0-0 10 ♕c2 h6 11 e4 ♘xc3 12 bxc3 c5 13 0-0 ♘c6 14 ♗b2 ♖c8 15 ♕e2 ♘a5 16 ♖ad1 cxd4 17 cxd4 ♗f6

see following diagram

This position has been assessed as unclear. White's centre pawns control four key squares in Black's half of the board and there is a potential passed d-pawn in the making. But this kind of space advantage is of a much different variety to the one we will see in the main game because here Black's forces enjoy some freedom, even exerting pressure on the centre pawns.

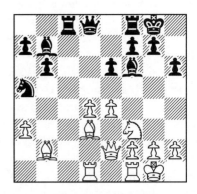

8 ♗b5+ c6 9 ♗d3 ♗g7 10 ♘a4!

Knights on the rim aren't always dim. I would hope that having read this far you are so in tune with your inner chess self that logical-looking moves and plans will be given a go even if they break conventional rules. In this case, after inconveniencing Black slightly by inducing ...c7-c6 White would like to keep the c6-pawn where it is and subsequently exploit his better centre and the territorial lead it provides. To do so means monitoring the c5-square, which gives us two candidates in 10 ♘e4 and 10 ♘a4. The former plants the knight in the middle of the board, which seems sensible enough but − thinking further ahead − obstructs the e3-pawn and so hinders development. With the text, however, ...c6-c5 is held at bay while the e-pawn is free to join ranks with the d4-pawn. The knight is on the edge of the board but everything has a price.

After 10 ♘e2?! c5 11 dxc5 bxc5 12 ♕c2 ♘d7 Black had the more active forces and an isolated c-pawn that afforded him more space in Lobron-Karpov, Dortmund 1995. Alternatively 10 e4 ♘xc3 11 bxc3 c5 12 ♗g5 ♕d6 13 e5 ♕d7 was equal in Kasparov-Korchnoi, London 1983 so, if White is to prevent the freeing ...c6-c5, the solution is almost made for him. A bonus feature of ♘a4 is the tempo about to be gained when hitting Black's knight with e3-e4 now that ...♘xc3 is not available.

10...♘d7 11 e4 ♘e7 12 0-0

The immediate 12 ♗f4 anyway allows 12...c5! as 13 dxc5 meets with 13...b5! 14 ♘c3 (14 ♗xb5? ♕a5+) 14...a6! 15 ♗d6 ♖c8 when Black has an edge.

12...0-0

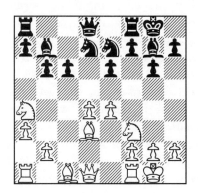

13 ♗g5

Khalifman prefers to keep Black under pressure. 13 ♗f4 c5 14 dxc5 ♘xc5 15 ♘xc5 bxc5 16 ♕e2 ♘c6 was level in the game Yermolinsky-A.Ivanov, USA Championship 1996, while 16 ♖c1 c4 17 ♗xc4 ♗xe4 is equal.

13...♖e8?!

In his notes to the game in his excellent book *Khalifman: Life & Games*, Gennady Nesis writes: 'Black's first 'in-dependent' move proves to be not very successful, and from this point White begins dictating matters.'

Incidentally, Khalifman-Short, Parnu 1996 was equal after 13...h6 14 ♗e3 ♔h7 15 ♖c1 f5.

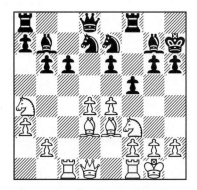

Note how Black had to be prepared to push his f-pawn in order to challenge White's centre. With the bishop on d3 and the king on h7 this might seem rather risky, and the e6-pawn has lost its support, but Black is well equipped to operate on the light squares and these potential problems are a small price to pay for the removal of the influential e4-pawn. Lesser mortals than Short (just about every player, then) would not only be concerned about pushing the f-pawn but would also be averse to spending two moves on placing the king on h7 in the first place, in the sights of the enemy bishop. Yet this would give White a free hand to build on his space advantage, in turn leading to an increasingly difficult game for Black.

Often it is possible to contest a territorial supremacy only by pro-active means that break 'rules' or look undesirable from a conventional viewpoint. In such circumstances the stronger player is far more likely to take a stand (rather than sit back) for two reasons: Firstly, he is well aware of the power of the space advantage and therefore the discomfort experienced on the 'wrong' side of the board in certain situations. Secondly, he is able to see the bigger picture when an awkward-looking move appears to offer the best prospects. Moreover, the fear factor in the first quality induces a necessary improvement in the second. A weaker player, on the other hand, has thus far in his career failed to properly acquaint himself with certain fundamental psychological aspects of the game, is less inclined to act accordingly (and therefore more inclined to drift into passivity) and is anyway less able to accurately weigh up relevant pros and cons.

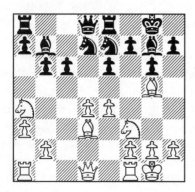

14 ⬜c1

Another piece homes in on c5.

14...♕b8

Nesis suggests 14...e5 15 dxe5 ♘xe5 16 ♘xe5 ♗xe5 17 ♕f3, when White still has a slight pull. In fact he believes this thematic freeing advance to be Black's last opportunity to have a say in the game.

15 ♗h4!

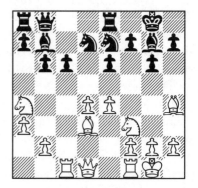

Exploiting the awkward posting of Black's queen, Khalifman drops his bishop back for relocation on the h2-b8 diagonal. In doing so the liberating ...e6-e5 thrust is addressed. Consequently both of Black's desirable, thematic pawn breaks have now been successfully prevented, giving White's territorial advantage a more long-term – and therefore – promising look.

Already in the diagram position Black is confined to only three ranks – his pieces no further than the second! I am sure that if the roles were reversed Khalifman would have refused to accept this position with Black. In fact it is quite possible that Sivokho himself would have played more energetically – 'breaking rules' to break out – with Black against an opponent considerably weaker than himself. Instead, perhaps intimidated, he settles for passive play.

15...h6

Shadowing the bishop with his own does not help Black: 15...♗h6 16 ⬜c2 e5 17 ♗g3 ♗f4 18 ♗xf4 exf4 19 ♕d2 etc.

16 b4

Threatening to push again to b5, which would practically force Black on to an awkward defensive after the trade on b5. Consequently Black's next appears to be a forced, albeit unattractive response.

16...b5 17 ♘c5 ♘xc5 18 ♖xc5

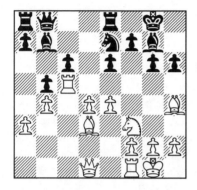

Black has had to kiss the c5-square goodbye, the c6-pawn is now backward and a permanent weakness and his forces have no future. Meanwhile White's advantage has increased. Thus far White had been concentrating on containing Black by doing nothing more than clamping down on the freeing ...c6-c5 and ...e6-e5. Nothing special, nothing aggressive – instead of trying to blow away his lower rated opponent Khalifman has relied on the positional pluses brought about by the opening.

Good positions play themselves, and White's prospects have improved along with Black's unadventurous play, to such an extent that the latest diagram position sees Black in danger of being dominated. Consequently Black seeks at least a semblance of counterplay on the queenside, where he is particularly cramped.

18...a5 19 ♘e5

It is significant that White now has a piece on each of the squares he was

trying to monitor earlier – and both in Black's half of the playing area. This is a sign that White's lead has taken on a new, more aggressive character.

19...♕d6 20 ♗c2 axb4 21 axb4 ♖a3

Black finally sends a piece into enemy territory but it is rather late and nowhere near makes up for his negative, passive play in the opening and early middlegame. White anyway stands better on the queenside thanks to the backward c6-pawn, has an undisputed command of the centre and the makings of a promising initiative on the kingside, where Black looks fairly solid but is unable to compromise his structure in front of the king. With this in mind White once again threatens to get busy with his dark-squared bishop.

22 ♗g3

Note that this bishop has done nothing out of the ordinary yet has nevertheless managed to create problems for Black through its mere presence. This time Black must retreat his queen from the 'advanced' post on the third rank, which highlights his unenviable plight. There are two major and related problems with passive, planless and what is essentially helpful, 'opponent-friendly' play – 1. The opposition is not presented with defensive tasks and (consequently) 2. The opposition is free to improve his game in a clear, calm manner. With little to worry about in terms of fielding threats or having to prepare for potential problems there is no sense of urgency for the player with the freer game to overplay his hand by unjustifiably trying to use his advantages. Instead it is better to play along with the opponent while he continues to put up little or no resistance to a gradual increase in pressure.

Stronger players like to have an input into a game and are afraid of giving their opponents too much freedom and flexibility. The average club player is less concerned with getting a hand on the steering wheel and begins to worry only when definite threats are made or when the opponent's attacking intentions are evident. Until there is something to actually respond to most players sit back too far, like a soccer team that is content to have all the players – including the attackers – in its own half of the playing field, thereby handing on a silver platter to the opposition the facility to be calm and collected and the luxury of being able to utilise more elements of the whole than is usual. But having an uncompromising edge and wanting a fair share of the board are not exclusive to strong players, and it is important to remember this the next time your opponent is having too much his own way.

On the other hand if you notice that your opponent is a little too accommodating it pays to let him continue, to let

his passive play work for you in the form of gradual, subtle improvements. An accumulation of ostensibly modest pluses can be just as effective as the more obvious ways of trying for an advantage.

22...♕d8 23 ♗f4!

Now the h6-pawn is the focus of attention.

23...♘c8

Nesis writes: Black has been completely outplayed, and all that is required of White is a certain accuracy in the conversion of his great positional advantage.

24 ♕c1 ♖a6 25 ♗xh6 ♕xd4 26 ♗xg7 ♔xg7

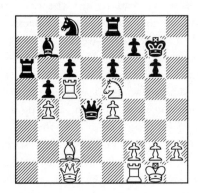

Black's best minor piece has left the board and he is left with the sorry looking bishop and back rank knight, while White's unwelcome visitors remain firmly in place on c5 and e5. Ironically the arrival of Black's queen on d4 might have lifted his spirits, but White is the one whose already healthy stock has risen in value during the last few moves. White's domination has afforded him the luxury of being able to step up the pace on his own terms, whilst Black's passive approach forces him to go along for the ride come what may. In fact the latest journey would have been rather short had White now played the consistent 27 ♕b1!, simply protecting the b4-pawn and preparing to infiltrate with ♖d1-d7 etc. I like these quiet but genuinely powerful moves. However, with such a lead it is understandable that Khalifman decides that now is the time to cash in on his lead, so he lets the b-pawn go...

27 ♖d1!? ♕xb4 28 ♕f4!

The point. Playing through instructive 'lessons' such as this game we are not surprised to see a territorial supremacy that is mainly on the queenside be ultimately converted into something concrete on the kingside.

The text will have served only to worsen Black's psychological state, for the discomfort and feeling of impending doom since failing to break out and earn a little breathing space with 13...h6 or 14...e5 has now been replaced by the stark reality of a lonely king. In contrast White has been enjoying all of the game, his latest show of aggression feeling perfectly natural.

Not once has White been inconvenienced. That is not to say White has ignored his opponent, rather that so little of his time has been taken up by checking over potentially troublesome lines (Black's set-up has not been conducive to such possibilities), leaving more time for his own agenda.

28...f5

28...♘d6 29 ♘g4 is decisive, while after 28...f6 29 ♘g4 ♕xc5 30 ♕xf6+ ♔g8 31 ♕xg6+ ♔f8 32 ♘h6! White will soon deliver mate.

29 ♕g5 ♘e7 30 ♘xg6!

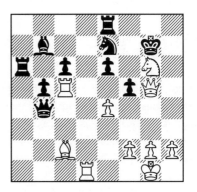

30...♕xc5 31 ♘xe7+ ♔f7 32 ♕g6+ 1-0

Nesis: 'The game is in general typical, in my opinion, of one where the rating difference is almost 300 Elo points. White wins without any outward effects, but simply by punishing Black for his imperceptible positional errors.'

Change of Pace

By now we should be well aware of how quickly and to what extent the flavour of a game can alter, whether this is a destructive sacrifice, a series of exchanges, a crafty double/multi-purpose plan in which a quick change of direction catches the opponent unawares, a subtle relocation of a hitherto dormant piece etc. While it is obviously impossible to 'prepare' for all such eventualities it is nevertheless worth bearing in mind that these things happen surprisingly often.

Being conscious of the 'unknown' is a form of mental preparation in itself and therefore leaves us more able to deal with this or that situation when the time comes. Just as my resignation to the fact that a walk through England's green pastures on a sunny June afternoon could well be accompanied by a rain shower or two, which prompts me to take along an umbrella, at the start of a chess day I should remind myself that I would be fortunate if things went according to plan on the board. However, a surprising number of people – even in England – simply fail to take the rain factor into account when setting off into the inviting sunshine with tee-shirt and shorts, only to be unpleasantly surprised by – and ill-equipped to deal with – any downward turn in the weather. The same goes for chess, which means we should be looking for opportunities to switch direction or change the pace of the game if it seems the opponent's sphere of expectation in terms of where the game might go is limited for one reason or another.

An effective way of suddenly putting the opponent under pressure is choosing an opening or defence that is considered rather harmless, and from behind which we can pounce with an injection of aggression that is considered unconventional or unusual for that particular line.

Here is a typical example in which White's choice of the ostensibly innocuous Exchange Variation against the Slav Defence leads to an early skirmish in the centre which leaves Black struggling as much as he would expect to in a more cut-and-thrust opening.

Illescas-Magem
Spain 1995
Slav Defence

1 d4 d5 2 ♘f3 ♘f6 3 c4 c6 4 ♘c3 e6 5 cxd5 cxd5

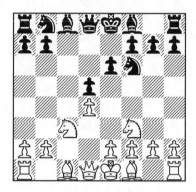

The recapture with the c-pawn is a particularly interesting and telling choice. Most players above a certain level would prefer 5...exd5 as this liberates the light-squared bishop and provides Black with a reasonable post for his king's rook on the e-file after the usual kingside castling. Instead Black has voluntarily left his bishop locked in behind the e6-pawn – an inconvenience that White does not have – and thus denied himself a freer game, accepting a symmetrical structure a tempo down in the process.

It is fair to assume that because Magem Badals opened with his first choice Slav he preferred to follow a course consistent with his tried and tested repertoire even when a supposedly more attractive opportunity presented itself. After all, White could have traded on d5 earlier, so if Black was prepared to follow that course then, he might as well stick with 'Plan A' a couple of moves later. Of course an on-the-ball GM with a 2550+ rating is quite capable of adapting to any number of situations as the opening progresses, and there is no doubt that such a well prepared player would be more than sufficiently acquainted with the theory. Consequently the text is simply part of Black's opening strategy and an indication that he is quite happy to defend the diagram position as per plan rather than change course to what is considered a perfectly playable game with the alternative recapture. 5...cxd5 fits in both with Black's style and game-plan. Taking these factors into consideration, it is interesting to briefly investigate what might have been going through White's mind during the first few moves here. The fact that he opted for 4 ♘f3 rather than 4 cxd5 suggests that he was willing to enter into the main lines which follow 4...dxc4 (5 a4) or take on the modern 4...a6. Was 4...e6 – introducing the possibility of serious complications in the event of 5 ♗g5 dxc4 6 e4 b5 etc. – a surprise to White, prompting him to turn down 5 ♗g5 and the less fiery but nonetheless potentially busy 5 e3 for the structurally safe trade on d5? Perhaps. Or maybe White did indeed expect Black's fourth move, anyway intended to exchange pawns and was putting out a psychological feeler, waiting to see how Black would respond. Whatever the respective intentions of the protagonists it is instructive to note the significance of each choice at each juncture, even after only a few moves!

6 ♗f4 ♘c6 7 e3 ♘h5?!

By no means rare, and most likely according to plan, but Illescas Cordoba believes this knight sortie is slightly inappropriate. It does seem that White's bishop will be reasonably posted on g5 or h4, whereas the knight will have to return to the fold at some point.

8 ♗g5 ♕b6

8...♗e7 9 ♗xe7 ♕xe7 10 ♗b5 gives White an edge despite the symmetry.

9 ♗b5 h6 10 ♗h4 ♗d7 11 0-0

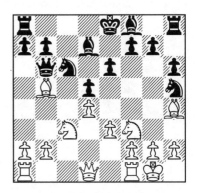

11...♖c8

At the time of the game this was a theoretical novelty, Black turning his attention away from the kingside in order to further the cause on the other flank. Baburin-Dreev, Gorky 1989 continued 11...♗d6!? 12 e4 (12 ♘e5 ♗xe5! 13 dxe5 g6 14 ♗xc6 ♗xc6 is equal) 12...0-0! (12...dxe4? 13 d5!) 13 exd5 exd5 14 ♘e5 ♗xe5 15 dxe5 ♘f4!? (15...d4) 16 ♗g3 ♘e6 17 ♕xd5 ♖fd8 (17...♖ad8!?) 18 ♕e4 ♘ed4 with an unclear position.

11...g5 has also been tried, e.g. 12 ♘d2 ♘g7 13 ♗g3 a6 14 ♗d3 ♗e7 15 ♘a4 ♕d8 16 ♘c5 ♗xc5 17 dxc5 e5 18 e4 ♗e6 19 exd5 ♕xd5 20 ♗e4 ♕d4 21 ♕f3!? as in Osnos-Nogueiras, Plovdiv 1982. The chief drawback of ...♖c8 here is the location of Black's king which, thanks to the bishop still being on f8, cannot quickly find safety by castling kingside. Consequently White decides to break the symmetry with a pawn break in the centre designed to catch his opponent's king unawares.

12 ♘d2!?

Hitting the 'dim' knight and therefore forcing some kind of structural concession from Black. 12 ♗xc6 ♗xc6 13 ♘e5 ♘f6 is equal according to Illescas.

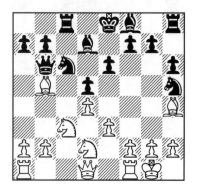

12...♘f6

12...g6 doesn't look right, so Black takes his chances in the central skirmish. Of course it is possible that Black was unaware of the e3-e4 pawn break in these positions, but it is more likely that he either underestimated its power or judged that his grip on the dark squares and what he thought was a sufficiently solid king position was enough to dissuade White from opening up the game. It is not unreasonable to assess the diagram position as unclear, but White – who has nevertheless instigated the change in pace – seems to better understand the new texture of the game.

13 ♗xf6 gxf6 14 e4

A long way from the ultra-solid, patient, perhaps even equal game that Black was looking forward to when he set out his stall with the Slav Defence! Now he finds himself just a dozen or so moves later standing toe to toe in the centre with an opponent who seems determined to deliver a knockout blow straight out of the opening. Top GMs

have secured their place in the higher echelons of the chess world because such a turnaround is really quite natural to them, but this does not mean that it is beyond the capabilities of the average club player to engineer similar situations.

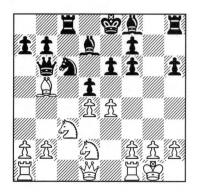

14...♘xd4?

After 14...dxe4?! 15 ♘dxe4 ♗e7 16 d5 White makes rapid progress as he cuts a path through the middle of the board. This leaves 14...a6 15 exd5 axb5 (15...exd5) 16 dxc6 bxc6!, when White enjoys the slightly better game after 17 ♘b3 f5!, with a few holes and a dodgy pawn formation in Black's set-up but some compensation in the form of the bishop pair and the isolated d4-pawn, or 17 ♘de4 f5!? 18 ♘f6+ ♔e7 19 ♘xd7 ♔xd7 20 ♕h5 etc.

Also possible – but appearing somewhat risky – is 14...♘b8!? 15 ♗xd7+ ♘xd7, e.g. 16 exd5 ♕xb2 17 dxe6 fxe6 18 ♘de4! ♖xc3 19 ♖b1 ♕a3 20 ♘xc3 ♕xc3 21 ♖xb7, when White seems to be doing well, or 16 ♘b3!? dxe4 17 ♘xe4 f5, which Illescas evaluates as a shade better for White.

The text is a natural, combative response but seems to help White more than Black.

15 ♗xd7+ ♔xd7 16 exd5 e5

16...♕xb2 17 ♕a4+ ♔d8 18 dxe6 ♘xe6 19 ♖fd1 is decisive.

17 ♕h5!

The pressure mounts, and already we would not be able to determine by looking at the latest diagram position that the game began as a Slav! While it is true that White – not surprisingly – is doing very well here, it will be interesting to see how Black copes with the defensive problems facing him. Imagine having this position with White in a game. I would expect most players to be more than happy to actually start the game here – including those who consider themselves to be steady, no risk, patient players who tend to shy away from anything approaching complicated even if the complications favour them. However, we don't find ourselves in promising positions by accident (at least not as often as we would like). They require some effort and a necessary willingness to occasionally engage the opponent in hand-to-hand combat somewhere along the line. Unless we are particularly adventurous or are (or think we are) attacking players, we will continu-

ally – and deliberately – take the 'safe' option. This is human nature and is a common characteristic at all levels. Many points or promising situations simply go begging, and many opponents are thus saved a potentially uncomfortable task. Yet, reversing roles, how many times are we trundling along nicely only for an uncaring opponent to shatter our illusion of security or of confident expectation by altering the course of the game in some way?

'I like to see them squirm.'
Bobby Fischer

Surely – what's good for the goose is good for the gander, so why can't we meter out the same treatment to other players? We recognise the nervous, uncomfortable feelings that are experienced when an unexpected turn of events is brought about by an opponent. (Remember that this change does not necessarily have to be drastic, just sufficiently significant to sow the seeds of doubt regarding our confidence in the ability to continue to conduct the game with the usual level of competence.)

Since we are concentrating on psychological aspects of the game it makes sense to put ourselves in the opponent's shoes and entertain the possibility that it is often worthwhile making the effort to unsettle him (before he unsettles us!). And it is by no means unfeasible to saddle the opposition with a generous helping of anxiety even if our opening repertoire consists of conventionally quiet lines or if our style is supposed to be safe and steady. A little discomfort for you might well cause much more concern for your opponent.

As they stroll around the tournament hall between moves some players like to stand behind their opponent to look at the game from the opposition's point of view, this second perspective providing an insight into how your contributions to the game might be received on the other side of the board. A course of action that you might consider inadequate because there is no concrete advantage or a line that results in an unclear position with chances for both sides could easily be viewed completely differently by the opposition, who is already at a disadvantage (you are in the driving seat, remember) and will initially be busy readjusting – a difficult process in itself – rather than analysing what is to follow.

Anyway, let us see how the game continued:

17...♔e8

Illescas also gives 17...f5!? 18 ♕xf7+ with the following lines: 18...♔d8!? 19 ♘b3 ♖c7 20 ♕h5 ♖g8 (20...♕f6 21 ♘xd4 exd4 22 ♖fe1!) 21 ♘xd4 exd4 22 ♖ae1! ♗e7 (22...♕g6 23 ♕xg6 ♖xg6 24 ♘b5) 23 ♖e6 ♕c5 24 b4! ♕c4 (24...♕xc3 25 d6) 25 ♕xf5 and 18...♗e7 19 ♘c4! (19 ♖ae1 ♕f6 20 ♕xf6 ♗xf6 is less clear) 19...♕f6 (19...♖xc4 20 d6 ♕xd6 21 ♕xc4) 20 d6! with a clear advantage to White in both cases.

Alternatively 17...♗e7 18 ♘b3 ♔e8 19 ♖fd1 is another line that is very good for White. In general we try to avoid leaving the king in the centre for too long, while voluntarily forfeiting the right to castle is even more serious. Stronger players do break more 'rules'

but the cause of Black's problems here is obvious.

18 ♘f3 ♖c4!?

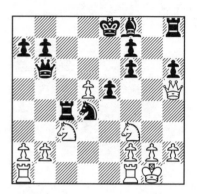

18...♖g8 eyes the g-pawn but adds weight to 19 ♘e4, while 18...♕xb2 predictably walks into trouble after 19 ♘e4, e.g. 19...♗e7 20 ♘xd4 ♕xd4 21 ♕f5 ♖c4 22 ♘xf6+ ♗xf6 23 ♕xf6 e4 24 ♕f4 etc.

19 ♖fe1

Another option is 19 ♘xe5!? fxe5 20 ♕xe5+ ♔d7 21 ♕xh8 when Illescas investigates 21...♘f3+!.

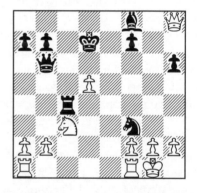

How do you think you would cope in this situation after having engineered the battle in the centre in the first place? 22 ♔h1? ♖h4 23 h3 ♖xh3+! 24 gxh3 ♕d6 25 ♔g2 ♘h4+ 26 ♔h1 ♘f3 leads to a draw, so critical is 22 gxf3 ♕g6+ 23 ♔h1 ♕h5 (23...♕f5 24 ♖g1 ♕xf3+ 25 ♖g2 ♖g4 26 ♖ag1 ♗g7 27 ♕b8 ♗xc3 28 ♕xb7+) 24 ♖g1 (24 ♕f6? ♗d6) 24...♗d6! (24...♖h4? 25 ♔g2! ♖xh2+ 26 ♔f1) 25 f4! (25 ♖g2? ♖h4 26 ♔g1 ♖xh2 27 ♖xh2 ♕xh2+ 28 ♔f1 ♕h1+ 29 ♔e2 ♕xa1 30 ♘e4 ♕xa2 31 ♘f6+ ♔e7 32 ♘g8+ ♔d7 33 ♘f6+ and 25 ♔g2? ♕xh2+ 26 ♔f1 ♗c5 27 ♘d1 ♖c2 28 ♖g2 ♕h1+ 29 ♖g1 ♕h3+ 30 ♖g2 both draw) 25...♖xf4 26 ♕a8!

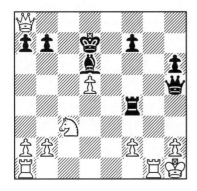

What a move. Lateral thinking! After 26...♖h4 27 ♕xb7+ Black's mate threat is irrelevant as his king will be caught first.

19...♗d6

19...♘xf3+ 20 ♕xf3 ♖g8 21 ♘e4 ♖g6 22 ♖ac1 ♖xc1 23 ♖xc1 is very much in White's favour but looks like a lesser evil to me.

20 ♘e4 ♔e7

20...♗b8 21 ♘xd4 ♖xd4 22 ♕f5 ♔e7 23 ♖ad1 ♖xd1 24 ♖xd1 ♖d8 25 d6+ ♖xd6 26 ♖xd6 ♗xd6 27 ♕xf6+ ♔d7 28 ♕xf7+ and 20...♘c2 21 ♘xf6+ ♔d8 22 ♘g5 ♖f8 23 ♘xf7+ ♔c7 (23...♔e7 24 ♘xe5) 24 ♖ac1 are decisive.

21 ♘xd4 ♖xd4 22 ♕f5 ♗b4

22...♗b8 23 ♖ad1 is awful for Black

so he prefers to add to the impression of activity by placing a second piece in enemy territory. A closer look at the layout of the respective forces, however, reveals that White's are optimally posted, and the next is not really a great surprise in coming.

23 ♘xf6!

Much stronger than the natural 23 ♖ed1. No doubt Black saw this coming, but since White inflicted on him significant structural damage with ♗xf6 and followed up with the logical pawn break in the middle of the arena Black's game has been difficult indeed.

23...♗xe1 24 ♕xe5+ ♔d8 25 ♖xe1 ♖c4 26 d6 1-0

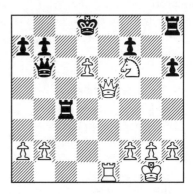

It is fitting that Black's king is the final target. After a very quiet start White's 12th move forced a positional concession from an opponent who had set his stall out for a solid game by opting for symmetry when a conventionally preferable alternative was available.

In the Grandmaster's Shoes

If we could somehow tap into a strong player's mind during a game to listen to his thoughts and emotions, the experience would be both interesting and in-

structive. Unfortunately this is not possible, so we can only play through their
games in print. Occasionally such games
feature annotations, but these tend to
focus on the latest theoretical developments, deep tactical variations or the
finer points of technical endings. Obviously we can learn a lot from studying
the games of top players, but a few can-
did remarks about various stages of the
game could be equally important.

In the next game we are able to sit
alongside GM Suat Atalik, whose com-
ments from the very first move provide
us with a useful insight into how these
players approach a game. It is significant that the notes (based on Atalik's
annotations to the game for *ChessBase*)
are generally along the same lines as our
own would be. The notes in *italics* are
my own observations.

Atalik-Halkias
Greek League 2002
Queen's Gambit Accepted

1 ♘f3

I wanted to catch him in his Tarrasch
rather than the Benko, that is why I
have changed my usual first move.

*Already Atalik puts some thought into how
the opening might pan out, avoiding the Benko
Gambit (1 d4 ♘f6 2 c4 c5 3 d5 b5) by
tweaking his move order.*

1...♘f6

Now my opponent surprised me
since after this it is obvious that we
won't have a normal Tarrasch.

2 c4 e6 3 ♘c3 d5 4 d4 dxc4 5 e3

I was reluctant to go for the main line
against the Vienna (5 e4 ♗b4 6 ♗g5)
since I had earlier had two headaches

with this line.

**5...a6 6 a4 c5 7 ♗xc4 ♘c6 8 0-0
♗e7 9 ♕e2**

I was happy with this move, expecting an equal position to grind the Greek
down slowly.

*Despite the unexpected course of the opening,
which saw him turn down the recommended,
aggressive 5 e4, White is nevertheless content
with the current position and has a clear plan
in mind.*

9...0-0

That was unexpected though. 9...cxd4
10 ♖d1 e5 11 exd4 exd4 12 ♘xd4
♘xd4 13 ♕e5 ♕d6 14 ♕xd4 (Black's
dark-squared bishop should be kept off
the b8-h2 diagonal) 14...♕xd4 15 ♖xd4
0-0 (15...♗c5 16 ♖d1 0-0 17 ♗g5) 16
♗g5!? is typical – these positions are
equal but still contain some venom.

10 ♖d1 ♕c7

Now we are in Dlugy's line. Maxim
used to play this position rock solidly...
During the Dutch Championship I had
many philosophical discussions in the
company of both white and red wine
with my new and former compatriot
GM Ivan Sokolov. I remember that the
wise man told me that things were not
that simple in his games against

Rublevsky and Shirov. At this point I decided to steer the game parallel to those games.

The efficacy of discussing theory while drinking (red and white) wine is doubtful, although the content of these discussions clearly left a mark somewhere in his memory!

11 dxc5 ♗xc5 12 ♗d2

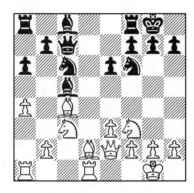

Mini move! Looks pretty dumb, huh? Of course many novices have played this without any understanding and without any pre-game conversation with Ivan.

12...b6

Everybody does this automatically. I was more concerned about 12...♘e5!, knowing from Rubinstein's games that both sides should be aiming to be the first to place a knight on e4/e5.

You will find very few Rubinstein games when studying the latest theory, so Atalik is now retrieving some genuine work from his mental library.

13 ♗d3! ♗b7

Played pretty quickly. My big idea was 13...♘e5 14 ♘e4! ♘xd3 15 ♘xf6+ gxf6 16 ♕xd3 ♗b7 17 ♗c3 f5 18 ♕c4.

14 ♘e4

Finally we have a position very close to Sokolov-Rublevsky, Poikovsky 2002.

This in itself will have been a satisfying achievement for Atalik, whose attempt to deny his opponent his usual defence was not entirely successful.

14...♘xe4 15 ♗xe4 ♖ad8

15...f5 16 ♗d3 (16...♘e5 17 ♘xe5 ♕xe5 18 ♗c3 ♕d5 19 f3, or 18...♕c7 19 ♗c4 ♕c6 20 ♕f3? ♕xf3 21 ♗xe6+ ♔h8 22 gxf3 ♗xf3 23 ♖d7) 16...e5 17 ♘g5 and Black has insurmountable problems.

16 ♗c3

16 ♗xh7+ ♔xh7 17 ♘g5+ ♔g6 18 ♕g4 f5.

16...h6

This little move could be useful. 16...♖xd1+ 17 ♖xd1 ♖d8 18 ♖c1! was in the boundaries of my thoughts.

17 ♘d2

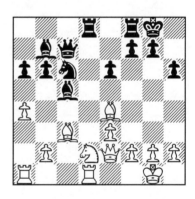

Before this move I stopped for a substantial amount of time. I really did not want to decelerate. However my original intention to carry the queen to the kingside runs into some tactics: 17 ♕c4 ♘a5! 18 ♗xa5 ♗xe4 19 ♕xe4 bxa5 with equality. And as usual I am always allergic to moves like 17 h3.

White checks through and subsequently opts out of his original plan but still wants to come up with something constructive, rather than the anyway sensible-looking h2-h3.

17...f5?!

Very aggressive. I had to be concerned about what would happen if my opponent burnt his bridges. 17...♗d6 18 h3 (18 ♕h5 f5; 18 f4 f5 19 ♗f3) 18...f5 (18...♗e5 19 ♖ac1) 19 ♗d3 ♘b4 20 ♗c4.

18 ♗f3

Justifiably very cautious. I was scared of some ballistic attack: 18 ♗d3? ♘e5 (18...f4?! 19 exf4 ♖xf4 20 ♕xe6+) 19 ♗xa6 ♗xa6 20 ♕xa6 f4 (20...♘g4? 21 ♘f3 ♖xd1+ 22 ♖xd1 f4 23 ♕c4!) 21 b4 fxe3!

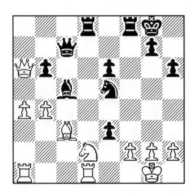

Regardless of how much of this Atalik saw it is clear that his sense of danger allowed him to avoid trouble, e.g. 22 bxc5 exf2+ 23 ♔h1 ♖xd2!! etc.

18...♔h7

Black has to mark time before the action. 18...e5? 19 ♕c4+ ♔h7 20 b4 ♗d6 21 b5 e4 22 bxc6 (22 ♘xe4 ♗xh2+ 23 ♔f1 axb5 24 axb5 ♘a5 25 ♕xc7 ♗xc7 26 ♘d2 ♗xf3 27 ♘xf3) 22...♗xh2+ 23 ♔h1 ♗xc6 24 ♗e2.

19 ♕c4

Finally the time has come to show some teeth. I was about to bring some imbalance to the position, practically

forcing the trade of h2 for Black's central e6-pawn.

19...♗d6!

What else? I had all the threats on earth: b2-b4 or a4-a5.

20 ♕xe6 ♗xh2+ 21 ♔h1

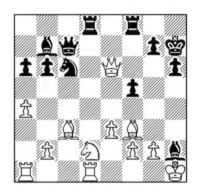

21...♖d6?

Playing with fire! Of course Black had alternatives. 21...♗d6 22 ♖ac1! favours White, while 22 ♘c4 ♗c8 23 ♕d5 ♘b4 (23...♘e7? 24 ♕d4) 24 ♕xd6 ♖xd6 25 ♘xd6 ♕e7 26 ♘xc8 ♖xc8 27 ♖d2 is less clear. After 21...♖de8 22 ♕c4 ♗d6 23 b4 (23 ♖ac1 ♖c8) 23...♖c8 24 b5 axb5 25 axb5 ♘e5 26 ♕xc7 ♖xc7 27 ♗xb7 Black must recapture with 27...♖xb7 because of 27...♖xc3? 28 ♘e4! etc.

This variation is impressive and had to be calculated during the game. The habit of analysing 'one more move' is a good one, in this case producing 28 ♘e4! in response to 27...♖xc3.

22 ♕c4 ♖e8

Stelios went very low on time before producing this. I was expecting 22...♖g6 23 g3 ♗xg3 24 fxg3 ♕xg3 25 ♕f4!?.

23 b4!?

All of a sudden I became steady at the wheel!

With his planned advantage materialising and his opponent running short of time, Atalik's confidence in his prospects are positive...

23...b5!?

The move I was considering to be the best. 23...♕b8? 24 ♕f7! was my idea. 23...♖d7 24 ♖ac1 ♗d6 25 b5 axb5 26 ♕xb5! is clearly better for White.

24 axb5 axb5 25 ♕xb5

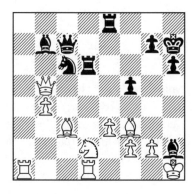

So finally I have won a pawn.

25...♗e5 26 ♘c4

Suddenly I became uncomfortable with my position for no reason at all and decided to go for this silly combination.

...But in the space of only three moves his grip on the wheel is not so steady! This stage of the game, with one player assuming the advantage and the other having to literally up the tempo of his moves while a lot of pieces remain on the board is critical. A clear advantage can quickly be transformed into a loss. Instead of the circumspect 26 ♗xe5 ♖xe5 27 ♕c4 ♕e7 28 ♖ac1, when White is well ahead and in relative safety, Atalik — like a boxer needing only to avoid trouble until the final bell — initiates unnecessary complications.

26...♖xd1+ 27 ♖xd1 ♗xc3 28 ♕xf5+ g6

I missed this idiotic move!

Idiotic? It is also obvious!

28...♔g8 29 ♖d7 and 28...♔h8 29 ♘d6 ♖d8 (29...♖e5 30 ♘f7+) 30 ♘f7+ (30 ♘xb7 ♖xd1+ 31 ♗xd1 ♘xb4 32 ♘c5!) 30...♔g8 31 ♘xd8 ♘xd8 32 ♖d7 ♕b6 33 ♖e7 ♗c6 34 ♗d5+! were easy to find.

29 ♖d7+

Now I had no choice but to go into a slightly better ending with an extra pawn.

29...♖e7 30 ♖xc7 gxf5 31 ♖xe7+ ♘xe7 32 ♗xb7 ♗xb4 33 f4!

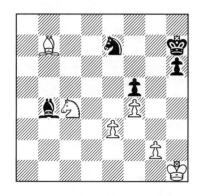

Here I pulled myself together and decided to play quickly and naturally to keep my opponent down to one minute on his clock.

The whole nature of the struggle has drastically altered but Atalik manages to quickly readjust to the circumstances and regain his composure, putting the onus to defend back on his opponent. His practical psychology is rewarded immediately.

33...♔g7?!

33...h5 is slightly better for White. Black should not be afraid of this.

34 ♔g1 ♔f6 35 ♔f2 ♘g6 36 ♔f3 ♘h4+ 37 ♔e2 ♘g6 38 ♗b6 ♘e7 39 ♗f3! ♗d6 40 g4 ♗c7 41 ♘d7+ ♔f7

41...♔e6 42 ♘c5+ ♔d6 43 ♘d3.

42 gxf5 ♘xf5 43 ♗g4 ♘d6

43...♘g7 44 ♔f3 h5 45 ♗h3!.

44 ♘e5+ ♔e7 45 ♔f3 ♘f7

45...♘b5 46 ♔e4 ♘c3+ 47 ♔f5 ♘d5 48 ♘c4.

46 ♘c6+ ♔f6

46...♔d6 47 ♘d4.

47 e4 ♘d8 48 e5+ ♔f7

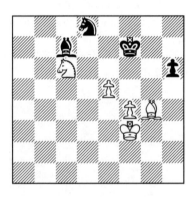

49 ♘d4!

Simply building up the position. It is too early to exchange knights: 49 ♘xd8+ ♗xd8 50 f5 ♗g5 51 ♗h5+ ♔e7 52 ♗g6 ♗d2 53 f6+ ♔e6 54 ♔e4 ♗g5! allows Black to put up more resistance.

49...♗b6 50 ♔e4 ♗c7 51 ♗h5+ ♔f8 52 ♔d5

52 ♘f5 ♘e6 53 ♘xh6.

52...♗a5 53 ♘e6+

The killer punch. With my pawns so far advanced, Black is dead.

53...♘xe6 54 ♔xe6 ♗d2

54...♗d8 55 f5 ♗e7 56 f6 ♗d8 57 ♔f5 ♔g8 58 e6 ♔f8 59 ♗g6.

55 f5 ♗c3 56 f6 ♗d4 57 ♔f5 ♗c3 58 e6 ♗b4 59 ♔e4 ♗a3 60 ♔d5 1-0

I have won this type of position even with an exchange down against GM Dautov in Ohrid...

Atalik can compare even this ending to one of his earlier games! Now there is an addition for the memory banks.

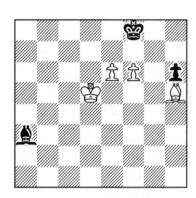

Imagine there's no Theory...

...It's easy if you try! Many players argue that computer databases have done away with creativity. Certainly this is an argument/excuse that I have been known to put forward when trying to explain away my increasing preference for the written word! This is what Yugoslav GM Ljubomir Ljubojevic – one of the chess world's most exciting and imaginative players – had to say about the subject in an interview a few years ago: 'My generation (Karpov, Timman, Miles...) fought at the chessboard – nowadays that job is being done by home analysis. The changes in chess concern the perfection of computers and the breakthrough of high technology. Under this influence the game is losing its charm and reducing more and more the number of creative players. Before, one played on intuition, feeling; now, technique, especially at the highest level, is more important...'

Of course some degree of work and effort should play a part in anyone's success, so the young players we see winning tournaments and getting the better of their older, more experienced rivals deserve credit for spending hours in front of a computer screen, number-crunching until their long-term memory banks seem full to the brim with an encyclopaedic level of theoretical information. This kind of dedication is no different to the good old days when a serious player would prepare for events (and specific opponents) surrounded by books and magazines. But today computers are considered an almost essential tool even for non-essential tasks; we are used to having them around – like a television or a compact disc player – and for children in particular a computer promises to make learning more interesting than a book, especially when sorting out literally thousands of games can be carried out in seconds. Perhaps this is progress, or perhaps it is a sad fact of life, but it is a fact of life all the same.

Because there is a vast amount of information available compared with, for example, the 1980s and earlier, so the focus of chess work has shifted to such an extent that theory seems to play a more important role even among club players. Again this is understandable but, unless you are a top player looking to break into the world's elite, a genuine understanding of the many aspects of 'real' chess is paramount. We do need to know some theory in order to avoid mishaps before we get a chance to actually play (and to see the opposition think for himself), but religiously downloading daily collections of games from the Internet to keep abreast of the latest trends is for budding world

champions only, and even then it seems to me to be rather extreme. Professionals feel professional doing this, but chess enthusiasts should feel enthusiastic about good old traditional things like structure, tactics, weak squares, the minority attack, good knight versus bad bishop endings and – as important as anything – themselves!

If we were not shackled by the restraints of modern day theoretical demands we could simply get down to a proper battle from the very first move! Let's see what you make of the following game, which is the opener from a 'Fischerandom' match in Mainz, 2001. In this form of chess the initial starting position of the pieces is randomly altered before each game. Thus the starting position for this encounter was as follows:

Leko-Adams
Exhibition Match, Mainz 2001

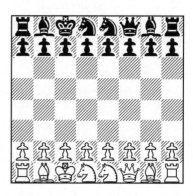

There you are – where's your opening repertoire going to get you now?! Before playing through the game it is worth considering your initial thoughts about the diagram position (after no more than 10-15 seconds) and then taking a closer, more detailed look, perhaps for a couple of minutes. Once you have become better accustomed to where the pieces are and how they might be brought into the game and so on, the situation will appear less unorthodox and less intimidating, albeit still rather awkward as soon as the time comes to come up with an opening move!

Anyway, here is how two of the world's strongest players coped in the opening game:

1 e4

Already we have an interesting choice. The pieces might not occupy the usual starting positions but the aim of the game is the same. Occupation of the centre, for example, is still part of White's plans.

1...e5 2 ♘d3 f5!

Exciting stuff! We're not used to seeing thrusting f-pawns so early in the game, but this aggressive move issues a logical challenge on the light squares in the centre. What concerns us here is how we would cope in tournament conditions without the safety-net of learned theory, with our pieces no longer occupying the same starting squares that we have grown accustomed to over what for some of us might be hundreds or thousands of games played, seen, read etc. Some players – and not just club players! – start to get hot under the collar just because they find themselves out of their usual lines, unable to see their forces settling nicely in their familiar posts in readiness for yet another friendly middlegame (that is not to say that these same players necessarily conduct either stage very well – rather that familiarity helps psychologi-

cally). To some extent we are all like this, but if you find that you are not too phased by the 'fish out of water' scenario then you will do well. Flexibility, or feeling fairly comfortable (or not too uncomfortable!) in what for you are uncharted or little explored openings or middlegames is not only a useful characteristic, it also makes for more enjoyable chess! Variety is the spice of life...

3 exf5

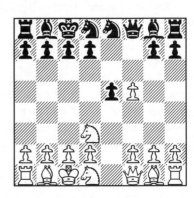

This appears odd given White's next move, but 3 ♘xe5 d6 and the immediate 3...fxe4 look nice for Black. At least the text will keep Black occupied sensibly recapturing the pawn.

3...e4

3...♕xf5? 4 ♘e3 helps White. We should all know to avoid bringing the queen into the game too early for fear of being given the run-around at the opponent's expense so, regardless of the odd situation we have been thrown into, we can use this to help round up the f5-pawn in the most effective way.

4 ♘e1 ♘d6

Hitting f5, supporting e4 and threatening to wade in with the bishop with ...♗c4.

5 ♘e3

Continuing in reversed King's Gambit style with 5 g4 leads to a second assault on the light squares after 5...h5.

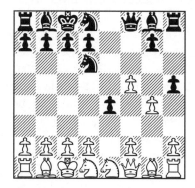

While we are conscious of the fact that the kings are sitting on the 'queenside' it seems odd nonetheless to look at the diagram position without thinking that these early pawn skirmishes on the kingside might prove a little risky... Then we look again and remember that this is not really the kingside after all.

The location of the rooks in their usual corner posts almost gives the position a semblance of normalcy, but the layout of the forces could well help create an impression that the middlegame has arrived after only a handful of moves. If this were the case in conventional chess we would have to be on our toes without delay in order to avoid being on the wrong side of an attack or to avoid suffering positional or structural damage, but the traditional starting position and the finite number of 'sensible' and known possible opening sequences affords us a certain level of security that enables us to at least manage quite a few moves before anything very bad happens out of the blue. Back in the 'real' chess world, if we try to play

with the same awareness and appreciation of the relationships of the pieces that tend to be required in the 'random' arena that is Fischerandom, then we will begin to see a lot more in our games and, consequently, learn more for the future.

That the likes of Leko and Adams can see the bigger picture is seen over the next dozen or so moves, for what is certainly an unusual position now soon looks completely normal...

5...♘xf5 6 f3

White justifies the lost time by now using the advanced e-pawn to further his own development.

6...♘xe3 7 ♗xe3 exf3 8 ♘xf3 ♗d5!

Black seeks to simplify and break White's 'h-side' pawns, as they are known. Notice how this latest position looks more 'familiar' than any other thus far.

9 c4 ♗xf3 10 ♕xf3 ♕xf3 11 gxf3 ♘e6 12 f4 c5!

Now it is Black's turn to release his bishop. What do you think of the way the game has been conducted so far? Would you have played along the same lines? Do you find the very nature of the unknown starting position off-putting or intimidating, or is it in fact a pleasant, refreshing change?

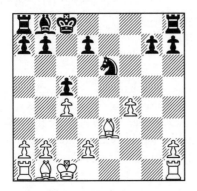

13 f5 ♘d4 14 ♗xd4 cxd4 15 ♗e4 ♗e5 16 ♔c2 ♔c7 17 ♔d3 ♖ae8

And this position is absolutely normal! In only seventeen moves since beginning the game from a bizarre starting position the super-GMs have survived the initial rough seas to steer the ship into the calm and friendly waters of a drawish ending. The fact that they were unable to follow their usual thorough preparation has proved to be of little relevance. White's next is designed to clamp down on the b7-pawn but Black is okay.

18 c5 ♗f6 19 b4 ♖e5 20 ♖he1 ♖he8 21 ♖e2 d5! 22 cxd6+

Not 22 ♗f3? ♖xe2 23 ♗xe2 ♖xe2 24 ♔xe2 d3+ etc.
22...♔xd6 23 ♖ae1 ♖8e7 24 ♗g2 ♖xe2 25 ♖xe2 ♗e5 26 h3 ½-½

Playing through this and the following game is a good indicator of your versatility, of whether you are 'at one' with your chess. Occasionally I suggest to my younger pupils who have just got into the habit – good or bad – of 'automatically' learning theory that they start the game with only the pawns and the minor pieces, or pawns, rook and knight or any other combination of forces that renders the Dragon or French and so on meaningless. At least this way they get to think for themselves from the off – and have a small enough collection of pieces to avoid blundering half of them away before the game gets going properly!

It is vital to get to know one's pieces, to understand the relationships they have with each other and with pawns. And like a soccer manager who continually tries to create a versatile, flexible team that can adapt to different circumstances and changing match conditions, a strong player has put enough thought into the game to recognise when it is time to give this or that piece (or unit of forces) an uncharacteristic role or task. These qualities are a key part of a strong player's armoury and facilitate a sensible, practical path through the opening stage. Kasparov and other top players are well known for their immense opening knowledge, but it is not unusual to see them deep in thought quite early in the game, perhaps suddenly questioning recognised theory and having to look for alternatives, or contemplating a re-organisation of the defensive forces through fear of a new idea in the coming middlegame etc.

The young pretenders who Ljubo-jevic might today label number-crunching and unimaginative could well possess a talent, an understanding of the game that seems way out of line with their age, that has even during such a short career also been shaped by hard work and psychological preparation. Over the years in my capacity as coach for England's juniors in world champi-onships I have spent time with a num-ber of very strong young players who have developed very quickly into strong GMs. Even as children these players looked and acted the part, and any pa-tronising opinions I had on seeing the strength of their opening preparation that this was the main ingredient of their medal winning success disappeared once I sat down with them and saw them analyse real chess. Now that you have seen the first Fischerandom game, and perhaps been a little confused by it, try to analyse a few other shuffled start-ing positions for a while until the ran-domness at the beginning does not look so odd. Then return to these pages and witness how two other GMs adapt to circumstances which, for professionals, would have been alien to them. Hope-fully the experience will be easier to understand despite the more combative route chosen by the protagonists.

Wojtkiewicz-Yermolinsky
San Francisco 2002

This time we have another starting position entirely, but the random factor is the same!

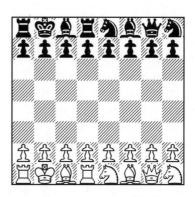

1 e4

In his thought-provoking book *Shall We Play Fischerandom Chess?* (where these games feature) Gligoric is interested in the opinions of his colleagues in the chess world about the pros and cons of 'shuffle' chess. He says that Wojtkiewicz claims that 'White holds a bigger advan-tage in Fischerandom than in regular chess as it is easier to grab the centre and get a spatial advantage...'

1...b6

Gligoric: 'Yermolinsky advocates a flexible attitude, believing that every piece configuration dictates its own strategy and that there is more than one of these for every set-up. He adds that "as a rule, instead of trying to rearrange your pieces into a familiar pattern, you should work with what is dealt to you." Here he thought fianchettoing the bishop was a neat idea, because it safe-guards the king.'

It is significant that it matters little whether 'Yermo' was talking about shuffle or conventional chess, for 'working with what is dealt to you' is a piece of advice we should all take note of. Like most good advice, though, most of us ignore it when the time comes, despite the fact that it is not always possible to have our pieces (re)arranged in a familiar pattern, and that familiar patterns aren't always the best. Rather than cut our cloth accordingly, making the best of what we have in a logical fashion that is specific to the situation, we become stereotyped.

2 d4 ♗b7 3 ♘g3 e6 4 f4 d5 5 ♗d3

5...♘g6

Black did not like 5...dxe4 6 ♗xe4 ♘d6 7 ♗xb7 ♔xb7 8 ♕f1 when White is ready to activate his queen on f3.

6 ♘f3

6 e5 is tempting because the traditional 6...c5? runs into trouble after 7 f5 exf5 8 ♗xf5, when Black's king position is more exposed than he would like. Instead 6...f5 7 exf6 ♘xf6 8 ♘f3 ♗d6 9 ♘e5 ♘e7 is unclear.

6...dxe4 7 ♗xe4 ♘d6 8 ♗xb7 ♔xb7

Again only eight moves have been played yet more seems to have happened than in a regular game. Notice also that both players have stuck to their respective game-plans mentioned earlier, with White rather insistent on establishing a grip on the centre and the

accompanying space advantage, while Black has been content to adopt a more positional, flexible strategy that can be tailored to his opponent's choice of 'opening'.

The previous game, while giving off an air of accuracy and control, began in interesting fashion but soon looked like a draw. Of course that had something to do with the strength and ultra-solid styles of the players involved and a psychological approach oriented to competing in exclusively world class tournaments. In the careers of Leko and Adams avoiding defeat is particularly important because the calibre of opposition is such that ostensibly very minor inaccuracies can lead to eventual loss. This safety mechanism has become such an essential part of their chess psyche that it manifests itself even when they face each other in 'shuffle' chess (against almost anyone outside the world's elite, on the other hand, I'm sure it would be a different story!).

In this game, however, we have two GMs who don't regularly compete with the likes of Kasparov, Kramnik and Anand but instead have to fight their way through big fields against some tough opponents, success being measured quite simply by the accumulation of points. This requires a more gladiatorial approach that in the long run has its foundations in a style that they feel best suits them. Of course as strong GMs they can be flexible, but in the most part they tend to be comfortable in certain situations. As we discussed earlier in the book it is important to know your 'chess self', to understand what makes you tick and so on. This takes time, effort and honesty, and is something that both Wojtkiewicz and Yermolinsky will have addressed. Consequently it is no coincidence that even in these quite different circumstances White's agenda is direct play and Black's is more practical, amorphous. If we have a sound psychological make-up we should be rewarded by the ability to adapt well, and this is demonstrated by all four players during the 'opening' phase in both games. Where the pieces started off has been of little consequence as far as effective development is concerned.

9 ♕f1

Gligoric gives the line 9 ♘e5 f6 10 ♘xg6 hxg6 11 ♕e3 ♕f7 12 ♕f3+ c6 as equal.

9...f6! 10 a4! a5 11 ♖a3

White utilises a mode of development for the rook usually seen at beginner level, although the end result is an effective set-up.

11...♕f7 12 ♖ad3 ♘e7

Looking at this position we wouldn't be surprised to learn that the game started out as a French Defence or maybe a Queen's Pawn opening, for example, with both sides castling queenside.

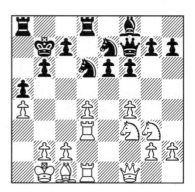

13 ♘e5?

Too direct! After 13 ♕e2 ♘d5 14 ♖e1 ♖e8 the game is level.

13...♕e8!

If 13...fxe5 14 dxe5 White is on top.

14 ♕f3+ ♚a7 15 ♖c3? fxe5 16 ♖xc7+

16 dxe5 ♘d5 17 ♖xd5 exd5 18 exd6 ♗xd6.

16...♚b8 17 dxe5 ♚xc7 18 exd6+ ♖xd6 19 ♖xd6 ♚xd6 20 ♕b7

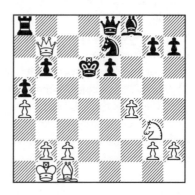

White threatens ♘e4 mate, but the extra rook is the key factor.

20...♕c6 21 ♘e4+ ♚d5 22 ♘c3+ ♚c4 0-1

Perhaps this form of chess is easier for the more so-called off-beat, individual players who are used to straying from 'main line' theory into unfashionable but sound lines that require more personal input than many modern day players are prepared for. What does seem to be the case in my experience is that the occasional experiment such as we had here (or simply starting the game with different combinations of pieces) serves to both prompt us to think for ourselves a little more and perhaps help in better understanding aspects of our chess psychology. It is also good fun!

The Chess Zone

In every sport the world's elite speak of the rare times – even for them – when all the important things seem to fall into place at the right time. Golfing great Tiger Woods would appear to have more than his fair share, holing putt after putt and driving the ball with super-human accuracy (not concerning himself with either the woods or the trees!). Olympic legend Carl Lewis at his peak could put together gold medal winning performances in both the 100 metres and the long jump in the same week! Michael Jordan, Michael Schumacher, Olga Korbut, Mohammed Ali, Pele, Babe Ruth... all these sporting greats had something in common – they found themselves in The Zone more often than their rivals.

We hear of the mystical Zone in sports films and read about it after great sporting achievements, and we marvel at the way just a few can out-perform the rest. I don't want to appear biased, but in my opinion chess is so complex that even the greatest players find their route to the zone paved with too many

obstacles. Perfection is probably impossible, but displays of brilliance illicit awe and emotion in genuine enthusiasts.

The Chess Zone is different to other sports, and is such that it is not beyond the reach of us mere mortals. Everybody has played what for them is a 'perfect' game, the only difference between us and Gazza is that he manages the feat more often, and against some of the best players in history. Even a short visit to the Chess Zone, just for a brief period during a game, can be enough to net the full point or to emerge unscathed with a draw with a fantastic defence when your king seems doomed.

There is no need to delve into the winner's psyche too deeply in our next game because it is enough to know that White seemed destined to win from the moment he sat down. His attack on the enemy king continued despite what seemed like 'abort' conditions. The fact that our hero is none other than the legendary David Bronstein explains why he was not going to allow the exposed position of his own king prevent him from producing a spectacular display. Bronstein was arguably the strongest player never to hold the title of world champion, and he is recognised by many to be one of the most exciting players in history. He knew of a place called the Chess Zone, and he had a season ticket.

Bronstein-Ljubojevic
Petropolis Interzonal 1973
Alekhine's Defence

1 e4 ♘f6

It is fitting that Ljubojevic sits on the

other side of the board, as he would have appreciated what follows. His choice of defence is typically provocative.

2 e5 ♘d5 3 d4 d6 4 c4 ♘b6 5 f4

White opts for the most ambitious response to the Alekhine, running the risk of over-extending his mass of pawns.

5...dxe5 6 fxe5 c5

More uncompromising, cut-throat play from the dapper Ljubo. Normally Black prefers 6...♘c6 7 ♗e3 ♗f5 8 ♘c3 e6, when after 9 ♘f3 the options are 9...♗b4, 9...♘b4?!, 9...♗g4, 9...♕d7 and 9...♗e7. The text is more fun.

7 d5 e6 8 ♘c3 exd5 9 cxd5 c4

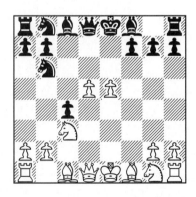

10 ♘f3

The theory is secondary here. *NCO* gives 10 d6 ♘c6 11 ♘f3 ♗g4 12 ♗f4 g5 13 ♘e4 gxf4 14 ♘f6+ ♕xf6 15 exf6 0-0-0 16 ♕c1! with a clear advantage to White.

10...♗g4

10...♗c5 allows 11 ♗xc4, while 10...♗b4! 11 ♗xc4 ♗xc3+ 12 bxc3 ♘xc4 13 ♕a4+ ♘d7 14 ♕xc4 ♘b6 15 ♕b5+ ♕d7 16 ♕xd7+ ♗xd7 17 d6 ♖c8 18 ♗d2 ♗b5 with compensation is a line I have seen somewhere.

11 ♕d4

Not 11 ♗xc4 ♘xc4 12 ♕a4+ ♘d7 13 ♕xc4 ♗xf3 14 gxf3 ♘xe5 etc.

11...♗xf3 12 gxf3 ♗b4 13 ♗xc4 0-0 14 ♖g1 g6

Earlier the game Ljubojevic-Honfi, Cacak 1971 went 14...♕c7 15 e6 f6 16 ♗h6 ♕xc4 17 ♖xg7+ ♔h8 18 ♖g8+!

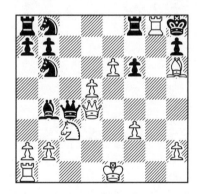

Then after 18...♔xg8 19 ♕g1+ Black was about to be mated. This experience enabled Ljubo to now play his moves instantly. However, according to an eye-witness: '...The following morning, Bronstein, after getting up early and with rapid steps setting off for a walk in the hills, left his hotel room holding a card with the text of the Ljubojevic-Honfi game, and showed it with his usual crafty smile. It thus remained un-clear when Bronstein had extracted this card from his index – before or after his game with Ljubojevic.' – We will never know, but Bronstein cannot have pre-pared for what follows in any case.

15 ♗g5 ♕c7 16 ♗b3

Damsky makes the interesting obser-vation that after 16 ♖g4 ♘xc4 17 ♕xc4 ♕xe5+ 'would have transformed the position from double-edged into a sharp one with chances for both sides. Or more precisely, a position where both sides are attacking.'

16...♗c5 17 ♕f4 ♗xg1

17...♘8d7 18 d6 ♕c6 19 0-0-0 ♗xg1 20 ♖xg1 ♕c5 21 ♖e1 ♖ae8 – Vasyukov.

18 d6

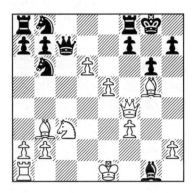

18...♕c8

'If 18...♕c5 I was planning 19 ♘e4! and after 19...♕b4+ 20 ♔f1 Black loses, while if he gives back a piece by 19...♕e3+ 20 ♕xe3 ♗xe3 21 ♗xe3 ♘c6 22 f4, then he remains material ahead but with a rather difficult position.' – Bronstein.

Nowadays we can simply open a book and be spoon fed the following variation: 19...♕d4 20 ♖d1 ♕xb2 21 ♘f6+ ♔h8 22 ♖d2 ♕a1+! 23 ♗d1 (23

♖d1 ♕b2) 23...♗e3!!.

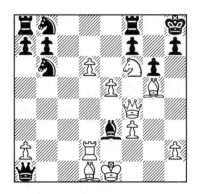

NCO continues 24 ♕xe3 ♘c4 25 ♘g4 f6 26 ♕d4 with an evaluation of 'unclear'...

Damsky gives 18...♕c6 19 e6 fxe6 20 ♗xe6+ ♔g7 21 ♗h6+.

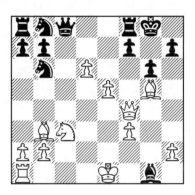

19 ♔e2?

'I wanted to retain the c1-square for my rook and freedom for my knight, but even so 19 0-0-0! should have been played, and if 19...♗c5! 20 e6 fxe6 21 ♕e5! ♖e8 22 d7! and wins.' But then Damsky gives 22...♘8xd7 23 ♗xe6+ ♖xe6 24 ♕xe6+ ♔g7, when White's attack does look inadequate, proposing instead 22 ♗e7.

19...♗c5 20 ♘e4 ♘8d7 21 ♖c1 ♕c6 22 ♖xc5!

There goes another rook.

22...♘xc5 23 ♘f6+ ♔h8 24 ♕h4 ♕b5+

Boris Vainstein, an old friend and second of Bronstein, wrote: 'A desperate sortie by the main forces, timed to coincide with White's time-trouble: Bronstein had less than one minute per move on his clock... There follows a final spurt by the white king, which, like Napoleon at the battle of Arcola, with a banner in his hand, went personally into the attack.'

25 ♔e3!!

The Zone! The Zone!

25...h5 26 ♘xh5

26...♕xb3+

'Black is forced to return all his gains,

as the pursuit of the white king by 26...♕d3+ 27 ♔f2 ♘e4+ 28 fxe4 ♕d4+ 29 ♔g2 ♕xb2+ 30 ♔h3 ♕c3+ 31 ♘g3+ ends in mate to the black king.' – Bronstein.

27 axb3 ♘d5+ 28 ♔d4 ♘e6+ 29 ♔xd5 ♘xg5 30 ♘f6+ ♔g7 31 ♕xg5 ♖fd8 32 e6 fxe6+ 33 ♔xe6

Of course White is winning by now, but the journey to the Zone has taken up so much of White's time that he had only seconds left at this point. (Bigger leads have come to nothing thanks to Father Time.).

33...♖f8 34 d7 a5 35 ♘g4 ♖a6+ 36 ♔e5 ♖f5+ 37 ♕xf5 gxf5 38 d8♕ fxg4 39 ♕d7+ ♔h6 40 ♕xb7 ♖g6 41 f4 1-0

'The entire 11th round was eclipsed by the quite fantastic game Bronstein-Ljubojevic, in which the veteran played with veritably youthful energy. In our time few are capable of playing such a game...' – Gufeld.

Imagine there's no Psychology...

...It's impossible. Unless you happen to be a computer. I am always self-satisfied when a computer loses to someone, as if I have played my own part in the victory just by being a fellow member of the human race, part of the team. However, the grim reality is that we will all lose in the end, as the following miniature – when a powerful computer program was allowed to participate in the 2000 Dutch Championships! – sadly demonstrates.

Van den Doel-Fritz SSS
Dutch Championship 2000
English Opening

1 c4 ♘f6 2 ♘c3 e5 3 e4?!

Perhaps not a wise choice against a piece of plastic.

3...♗c5 4 g3 0-0 5 ♗g2 ♘c6 6 ♘ge2 d6 7 d3??

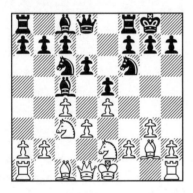

According to GM Luther, Fritz leaves 'his f6-knight on its square and allows himself to be boxed in' after 7 0-0.

7...♘g4 8 0-0 f5 9 ♘a4 ♘xf2!

The end is nigh. I don't like to think what was going through White's mind here. Black, of course, has no mind.

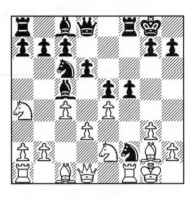

10 ♖xf2 ♗xf2+ 11 ♔xf2 f4 12 gxf4 exf4 13 ♘g1 ♕h4+ 14 ♔f1 f3 15 ♘xf3 ♕xh2 0-1

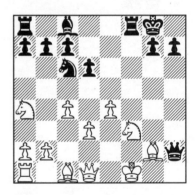

Let us hope in the future, dear reader, that there is a way to use your psychology to overcome computers. If not, you can always switch the power off.

Good luck.